PRAISE FOR TRUST CALL

"I have worked closely with Ryan since the early stages of his journey in developing the H2H Method and writing *Trust Call*. This has provided me with a unique opportunity to not only see how the years of experience, data, and phone calls have helped him refine his approach to cold calling, but also benefit from the knowledge he has gathered and shared with me. I always considered myself pretty good at sales but struggled in cold messaging, relying mostly on using whatever came to mind. I now have a starting point and a framework that I can use. I highly recommend *Trust Call* for anyone looking for an easy-to-follow guide to crafting and developing an effective message that will make a positive impact on their sales process."

— DENNYS DELGADO, SENIOR VP AT SHP

"For any business looking to harness the power of person-to-person sales calls, *Trust Call* offers a unique and valuable perspective on how to drive revenue through outreach strategies. I have personally experienced the benefits of this crucial mindset as a client of Ryan's for the past 3 years. The results are black and white, the strategy is proven and shows results, and any business can benefit from reading this remarkable book. There are mundane "cold call" strategies and then there is *Trust Call*."

— KEVIN FEIN, VP STRATEGIC SALES
AT MOEN

"So many sales books are based on theory. What makes *Trust Call* so compelling is it's built off of concrete data of what works and what doesn't. The methodology is also proven across all industries. This book is extremely practical and a must-read for any sales professional trying to find and close more qualified sales opportunities."

— BLAKE JOHNSTON, CEO & FOUNDER AT
OUTBOUNDVIEW

"For decades, cold calling has functioned with the same care as a drunk frat boy about to try an early morning balcony backflip. Shout, "YOLO," take the leap, and brace for pain because you know it isn't likely to end well. *Trust Call* challenges this reckless business practice and breathes new life into an activity that has remained largely unchanged for longer than most readers of this book have been alive. We have sophisticated processes and systems for engaging customers in every other stage of their decision journeys, yet when it comes to making initial contact with a prospect, we've stooped to essentially advising salespeople to do the wrong thing with such vigorous frequency that eventually they can win the "numbers game." No, call me idealistic, but we should be trying to do the wrong thing less often, maybe even never! *Trust Call* tells us we need to do better. More than that, it shows us how to do better."

— DR. WILLY BOLANDER, PROFESSOR AT
TEXAS A&M AND HOST OF THE SALES LAB
PODCAST

"Ryan Pereus is a cold calling legend who has created and scaled one of the top outsourced sales development firms in the world doing things the right way by delivering for his clients and earning their trust. This book is a breath of fresh air and offers an intriguing approach to the sales profession and cold calling. Ryan breaks down his philosophy to a tee, provides real data to back up, and gives us examples that we can use immediately. This is a must-read for anyone in sales or looking to get in sales."

— JOSH WILLIAMS, FOUNDER AT WILLIAMS
SALES AND BUSINESS DEVELOPMENT
INCORPORATED

"As a fledgling business in a new industry, we needed our sales lead process to be efficient and yield results while maintaining a high level of brand integrity. The H2H Method, coupled with Superhuman's team, immediately impressed. The script development process and the versatility of this sales method empowered a diverse call team, enabling us to win new B2B relationships in a modern marketplace."

— BEN AND KARAH DAVIES, OWNERS AT
WILD FOX PROVISIONS

"The H2H Method for Cold Calling has elevated my cold calling prowess to an elite level. I subscribe to the method because it's a successful sales strategy for every industry we call [FOR SUPERHUMAN PROSPECTING]. The reason I have set so many sales appointments for so many different companies in so many industries is because the method provides me with a process for selling. This makes it easy to adapt to new products I call while also maintaining quality."

— PATRICK BARD, 5 YEAR CLIENT SDR AT SUPERHUMAN PROSPECTING

"I first learned the H2H method as an SDR starting in 2021. As I entered into the cold calling world with a history in sales, I feel very strongly I have been able to develop both professionally and personally in the human-to-human methodology and skills from using the trust umbrella and following the script to the T. It not only taught me how to use my own natural tone and personality to converse in an effective manner, but also helped refine me as an individual. In former positions, I was never able to grasp what the cold call truly could be. In confidence, I will use this methodology for the rest of my career in sales and training. You will not be disappointed when you read *Trust Call* and I hope you grow to love the H2H methodology and the love of cold calling just as much as I have!"

— MERRY SYLVER, CORPORATE SDR TRAINER AT SUPERHUMAN PROSPECTING

TRUST CALL

RETHINKING TRADITIONAL TACTICS FOR A
HUMAN-TO-HUMAN CONNECTION IN COLD
CALLING

RYAN PEREUS

STREAMLINE BOOKS

CONTENTS

SECTION THREE
PRINCIPLES
UNLEARN AND REFRESH

SECTION FOUR
GET PRACTICAL, GET TACTICAL

SECTION FIVE
EVOLVING FUTURES WITH H2H

FOREWORD

BY REX BIBERSTON, FOUNDER
AND CEO OF NO FLUFF
SELLING

"This is the only call script you'll ever need."

I innocently took the single sheet of paper from my new manager's hand and sat down at my desk.

After just thirty minutes and a couple of conversations with strangers, I crumpled up the paper and started working on my own messaging.

As a young Business Development Representative at a fast-growing tech company, I had little idea what I was doing. But something inside me said that the "one size fits all" approach to cold calling wasn't the best path forward.

I went online, reading article after article, searching for the answer to a better cold calling script.

What I found was more of the same. One size the author claimed would fit all calling scenarios.

"Never ask someone how they're doing—it's disingenuous."

"Always ask buyers how they're doing—it's friendly."

"Always start with the purpose of your call."

"Never say the phrase, 'The purpose for my call is . . .'"

"Tell them it's a cold call and ask if they want to hang up or if they'll give you 30 seconds."

"If they ask if it's a cold call, say you're following up on some correspondence."

I never did find the right answer.

Instead, I picked up the phone and got to work. I called, and I spoke, and I failed. Then I called, and I spoke something different, and I succeeded. Little by little I crafted a consistently effective script that worked for me.

It worked so well I tripled quota in my third month (when others in my hiring class were still ramping).

But when those same reps tried to use my script, it never worked quite as well.

Since that time, I've made hundreds of thousands of phone calls to potential customers, trained hundreds of BDRs, SDRs, and the like, and owned two outsourced sales agencies that specialized in cold outreach.

I've spent a long time thinking about what made that script from my first BDR job successful for me where it failed for others.

This book makes it obvious.

There was no magic in my script. This wasn't the holy grail of cold calling. I had simply been applying lessons that I grew up learning from my father, a 20+ year enterprise sales veteran.

How he treated others.

How he respected the sales profession.

How he approached sales conversations with open-mindedness.

It all added up to a fundamental, deeply ingrained under-standing of why we cold call and how to talk to strangers in a way that disarms them and creates a moment of authentic connection.

What I learned from repetition, failure, and iteration is item-ized, named, and demonstrated brilliantly in the H2H method. If my first manager could have handed me this book instead of that single sheet of paper, he would have saved me a lot of headache (and made me a lot more money).

If you're reading this book, you might find yourself hunting through the pages hungrily searching for exactly what to say on your next call. The lessons that lie within do more than other books that simply feed you a fish you'll be sure to get sick of. Rather, Ryan lays out the deep roots of cold calling, why it's lost its shine, and how to turn the average seller's reluctance to make a dial into your advantage.

If you pay attention, he'll teach you how to fish. And hunt. And farm.

And when you turn that final page, you'll find yourself picking up the phone and making change happen for the buyers whose problems you can solve.

Happy selling.

TRUST CALL

"The only real objection that they have is that they don't trust you guys. And why should they trust you? I mean, look at you. You're a bunch of f***ing sleazy salesmen, right?"[1]

— LEONARDO DICAPRIO AS JORDAN
BELFORT, THE WOLF OF WALL STREET

SECTION ONE
PUT ON YOUR PHILOSOPHER CAP

For this first section, I want you to put on your philosopher cap. We'll talk about what H2H Method™ is, and then zoom out and talk about why it works. We'll talk about its importance in twenty-first-century relationships between seller and potential buyer.

As we go, think about some of the high-level concepts behind the cold call—in every single action we take. If we can zoom out like this, we can see the big picture and understand what's happening from a thirty-thousand-foot view, no matter what type of cold call activity we're engaged in.

CHAPTER 1
THE PROBLEM

PERSONAL ANECDOTE

Cold calling saw its heyday in the 1970s and 1980s. Unfortunately, so did boiler-room scams and bunk investment firms that regularly sold fraudulent products and services. By the time the U.S. Securities and Exchange Commission (SEC) cracked down on all the rampant, unethical practices, the damage to consumers and businesses had been done. The problem wasn't that people hated receiving a cold call (although that's what naysayers would have you believe). It was that trust between caller and prospect had been willfully and flagrantly broken.

The unfortunate stigma around cold calling has persisted to the point that cold calling *itself* is considered by many in the industry to be "all but dead." But what's killing it goes beyond fraudulent products and services. The stigma is deeply embedded in the strategies, tactics, techniques, and sales personalities of cold calling, and it's wreaking havoc on this sales profession subgenre. Even if products are true and quality, cold call execution is tarnished by its practice of justifying the means by its end. And, let's face it: We've all heard of the "slimy" or "sleazy" salespeople, "used car salesmen," and "swindlers" who continue to reinforce cold calling's bad name.

In my first sales job out of college, I experienced this firsthand. We were asked to do whatever we could to win a "yes" from the prospect, even if that meant lying, coercing, or slighting them. We were offering a good product, but that didn't matter, because we were breaking trust with prospects and potentially encouraging them to make a decision they could regret.

This is when my sales existential crisis kicked in. I was good at cold calling, and I enjoyed it. But I couldn't escape the dark cloud of what I thought of as *professional sales sin* hanging over me.

I took some time away from the profession to reflect, and an idea slowly took shape. Was the profession of selling truly "sinful" in nature, or were a few bad apples poisoning everything? Had cold calling truly stalled out, or could there be a way to push back against the riptide that was holding back what was truly good for the marketplace? I decided there was. Cold calling's honor, relevance, and efficacy needed to be restored. H2H Sales Scripts® and The H2H Method™ was found in this place.

But in early 2017, when I started the outsourced sales development service that is now a 45-employee operation at Superhuman Prospecting® (SHP) at the time this book was written, I didn't want to do it. I thought I would much rather spread the message of a new way to cold call in the twenty-first century through consulting, speaking, and writing. How could I impact the art and science of cold calling to the same degree that Zig Ziglar, Jordan Belfort, Grant Cardone, Jeb Blount, or Mike Weinberg had impacted the sales profession? It was an admittedly lofty goal, but one I felt I could achieve.

With my limited background at the time, however, not much was going to happen with my consulting career, at least for a long while. The longer I thought about it, the more lackluster my resume seemed. My experience was limited. My cold calling and sales appointment skills were above average, sure—but how would that help me transform an entire industry?

As I faced my reality, the truth in my gut started creeping up my throat, then finally into my head: If I wanted to truly debunk the stigmas placed on cold calling, reframe what it means to be someone who makes cold sales calls to strangers, and be an expert on actually knowing which cold calling strategies work and don't work across multiple industries and product or service offerings, there was an unavoidable journey ahead. I would have to learn—and master—what quite possibly no one else has: how to successfully cold call for virtually every major industry and have the relevant strategies and data to back it up. In essence, I would need to search long and hard to learn how human beings connect to product and service value through cold calling.

I hypothesized that if I could do this—learn how to cold call effectively for dozens of products and services spanning dozens of major industries—I might be onto something. A new methodology could shift the paradigm of modern cold calling away from its reputation as a tainted, stagnant, and beaten-up profession.

But how would this happen? How would I garner the opportunity, lessons, and data to confidently share with the sales community what my instincts were telling me all those years ago: cold calling is an honorable, brilliant, impactful job with the potential to change businesses for the better?

After all, that lump in my throat that kept me from going into consulting on my own was, ironically, what I knew was wrong with the sales improvement industry. At that point in my career, I'd had two or three jobs with good sales experience. As a sales professional, that was enough—but if I went into consulting, my learning would be considered middle-of-the-road and not enough to be confident in the impact. Like most consultants whose careers never get off the ground, my experience was far too little.

Many in the sales improvement space start by selling only a handful of products. Then, when they have success with one or three offerings, they attempt to replicate their results across all industries at a massive scale. It's a natural and organic development for many consultants, who help businesses in extraordinary ways, and it can even be a fast track to an independent career. However, it also creates a ceiling for these same professionals that limits them though their lack of cross-industry knowledge and global connections to larger theories. Without intentional research and networking, this is pretty much unavoidable. Sales has never been normalized as a discipline, and no one comes into their career already knowing everyone and everything in the industry. The result is a lot of self-proclaimed experts who are limited by virtue of the fact that they are drawing from their personal experience in a limited fashion. Unfortunately, placing expert titles before learning acquired is the same thing as putting the cart before the horse.

That's where I knew I may be able to help. If my focus was across multiple industries with a large data set, with time I could identify macro themes unprecedented in the sales development space. The learnings just might give me enough to scale my practices with confidence.

THE SOLUTION

It feels like there are an unlimited number of lessons learned that can be applied across industries. These truths apply to cold calling at levels from philosophy to frameworks. But there is one natural law surpassing anything else identified in my studies, and I will give you the answer before we even start the class. The natural law identified is that everything we do in a cold call with our prospective buyers has to work towards building trust. Otherwise the call can get off track, leading us away from the high-level results we're looking for.

Achieving those high-level results starts with building trust in everything. But to do that, we need to do our homework. First, we have to identify the strategies or objectives of a cold call, so we'll know the best things to say and do while on the call. To make effective use of that information, I developed the 4CX4 metric, or the Four Core Components of a Call, to help us identify the purpose of every piece of the conversation, so that we'll know what's coming next in our conversations with prospects. Finally, we have to test what we've learned by scaling across dozens of industries.

What better way to absorb, learn, refine, test, and repeat than to actually perform cold calls for, well, everyone? Cross-industry success meant reaching *all* humans in business. In 2017, that was the giant I had to face. To transform cold calling for the better and spread the message effectively, I would have to master a combination no one else had: the best market, the best message, the most relevance to products, and the best sales talent to execute and improve results for wide-ranging companies—all while the masses screamed "cold calling is dead." (In the coming pages, I'll discuss all the forces at play which work against cold calling, such as the idea that "content is king.") I would have to teach my recruits that every sales audience has a specific set of needs. Attempting to sell the same way to a school official and to a group of auto mechanics isn't likely to generate success. The same methods hit differently with different people; they have different impacts. That's why it's so important to identify any separation between the product and the selling.

Enter SHP, our team of U.S.-based superhuman professionals, dedicated to running outbound sales development campaigns for hundreds and hundreds of clients. Since its inception in 2017, we've made over a million cold call dials to potential prospects in multiple B2B and B2C industries.

Within two years we were able to aggregate the raw data from those calls and introduce H2H Scripts Scripts® and The H2H Method™. Part philosophy, part practice, it is pervasive and cemented in the structure of SHP's success. It is also a manifesto born from the formerly powerful, eventually disenfranchised, yet still timeless human-to-human method of bringing products and services to market: cold phone calling.

Welcome to twenty-first-century cold calling: a revolution, joined by droves of salespeople across multiple industries who are intent on reclaiming the lost art, but in a new way, founded in trust.

This is the mission of H2H Sales Scripts®. H2H stands for

human-to-human; all the philosophies, mindsets, strategies, and tactics in this book are built on creating and respecting a foundation of trust with prospects, with ourselves, and with the products and services we represent. It's an entirely redefined way of speaking with people that illuminates a better path forward: obtaining the best results possible, without sacrificing trust with potential buyers.

This book is a theoretical and practical guide on how humans connect to products and services in the twenty-first century through cold calling. Used by cold callers across the globe, and specifically by our team over at SHP, the methods in this book reflect the work done through thousands of hours and hundreds of thousands of calls made over a six-year period and counting. Whether you're looking for the best results possible when converting cold dials to warm leads, sales appointments, or seeking ideal next steps in the sales development "top-of-funnel," they define and redefine how to speak to cold prospects, regardless of industry.

I'm beyond thrilled to share these discoveries and help you repurpose your mission as a salesperson. My intent is to give power to the cold caller, so when faced with objections, doubt, negativity, and disrespect during activities, this book will be a light that helps make the next dial and another step in belief transference with your prospect. You know what your product or service can do for others, and you're holding the tool that will help you impact your audience in such a profound way that they'll change the course of their decisions and move towards the value you provide.

Let's go!

WHAT TO EXPECT

Let's set the first expectation for this course loud and clear:

WARNING! Cold calling can be HARD!

It can be *extremely tough* to get into those first cold phone calls with your prospective buyer. Often when we're in those first cold calls from zero to one, it can feel like we're underground. It can appear we're starting in the negative with people they don't yet trust—and frankly, for good reasons.

However, my hope is to give you strength (and give the prospect trust) by framing a new perspective. Not only will you learn how we've found cold calling works in the twenty-first century, you'll also learn how to achieve high-performing results compared to industry averages. After that, simply picking up the phone should no longer be a hurdle. Instead, we hope you'll start to see it as a puzzle or sport you excel in. Difficulty may be ever-present, but you'll be poised enough for anything thrown at you.

So what else can you expect? Here are a few things we hope you will glean from reading this book:

First, we hope to instill a new perspective on the cold phone call. When we consider the cold phone call, we think about *every single word we say* and how it fits within our philosophy and method. Every time we speak to a potential customer, we listen to what the prospect is saying and intentionally craft our response around it in that vital conversation from zero to one.

Second, we also hope to give you a new appreciation and respect for the *craft* of cold calling. Make no mistake: viewing cold calling through this lens will help you achieve better results. The more you can relish the process, the more you can enjoy the conversation and experience success. You'll see the benefits of your new appreciation, and so will your prospects. To get there, we're also going to breathe new life into some timeless tactical approaches. In fact, any twenty-first-century cold phone call conversation will bear some similarity to H2H. However, it's our structure—our outlook on every word, phrase, strategy, and purpose—that sets The H2H Method™ apart. Since the cold call requires such precise execution to be successful, all communication surrounding it needs to be scrutinized.

Lastly, you will learn bonafide strategy and tactics for your cold phone conversations. You will learn the bones of three different conversation structures, tactics within the steps of each, and other characteristics of a conversation to ensure what we say aligns with our overarching purpose. Learning these things will provide you some real, foundational takeaways to help you increase your appointment-setting rate and lead-setting rate on the number of dials you make after reading this book.

The more that you understand the purpose of a cold call and how it works, the more that you'll have that appreciation and respect, which will give you the driving endurance and skills needed to get the results you're looking for.

Going the distance for results is a critical mentality for success in cold calling. Think of it in terms of intentional, long-game learning that helps you accurately and consistently hit your target. Jim Collins' book *Great by Choice*, his followup to *Good to Great*, fantastically illustrates this principle. Collins takes a deep look at what made some of the top-performing companies in the world so successful. One of the tactics he discusses is a model each of these top performers tended to use in their business, which he calls "Fire Bullets, Then Cannonballs."

Collins says if you're in battle at sea, and there's an enemy ship, using all of your ammunition to fire a big cannonball at the target wouldn't be your wisest, first move. Why? Because if you miss, the enemy ship is going to know where you are, and you don't have any more ammunition to fire back again. However, if you start small and fire bullets first, you can begin to calibrate. For instance, if you fire once and miss, you can recalibrate and fire again. You'll progressively move a little closer and a little closer until you start hitting the target. Once you have calculated and have proof you can hit the target, you can then use a cannonball with more ammunition.[1]

Collins' method is an extremely effective guide for how to properly execute cold call strategy. In other words, your target, your message, and your script don't end the way they start.

When we're out there cold calling, you can also use the "Fire Bullets, Then Cannonballs" approach as a consistent learning cycle over the long term. With the methodology we've developed here, you're going to be firing bullets before cannonballs constantly as you use the feedback from each call to make micro-adjustments along the way. When you do this consistently, your process will improve and so will your results.

WHAT THIS BOOK IS NOT

- This book is not focused on B2C markets. In other words, much of the work, data, and research is derived primarily from B2B experience. The people we typically have and do call are within a company, organization, or government entity rather than homeowners or consumers directly. Some cold calling experience is gleaned from B2C industries, but more than 95% of the work is B2B.
- This book is not about finding motivation to cold call. While mindset and perception of cold calling is discussed in this book, finding the inspiration and drive specifically is not.
- This book is not a collection of suggestions, but a specific collection of connected ideas recommended to build in your muscle memory. The presupposition here muscle memory enables a base to move creatively and freely with all the foundations and rules set before it.
- Not a flood of tips, tricks, techniques. There is an immense amount of cold calling content in the world focused around openers, one-liners, quick-scripts, tricks and techniques. There are Linkedin posts, books, blogs, and videos on the topic. However, there is minimal work on the foundations of cold calling as a basis for building. This book focuses on these foundations so tips, tricks, and techniques can be applied to not only be effective, but continue building trust with prospects.
- This is not a book on how to execute well. There are certainly applicable execution topics covered here, but another full layer of cold call success can be attributed to

how the student executes the material learned. Michael Jordan or Lebron James could all teach us the foundations, strategies, and tactics of basketball, but that doesn't make us candidates to be in the GOAT argument. Execution is in practicing, role playing, gaining feedback, and try-try-trying again.

WHO IS THIS FOR?

Before we open the door to the method, let's identify some qualifiers. Who is this book for? In terms of title or position, this book can help the following:

- **Sales Development Reps (SDRs).** Those individuals who, whether part-time or full-time, are actively performing sales development activity (ie, cold calling) for the top of a sales funnel at their organization
- **Account Executives.** Those company team members who actively pursue full sales-cycle operations from sales development activity to deal closed
- **Sales Managers.** Those management team members who oversee and drive the performance of SDRs or account executives teams
- **Vice Presidents or Sales Leadership**. Leadership individuals who develop, make decisions on, and implement sales processes and strategy at their organization
- **Entrepreneurs or Small Business Owners**. Founding members of organizations who need to design and also implement outbound sales systems to grow at scale

Anyone in these positions can benefit from this book. Used either while calling, training team members on how to cold call, or implementing a system for their teams to call, this book provides a foundational basis for scaling cold calling not found in publicly available books.

In terms of company profile, here are a few company type qualifiers this book will benefit:

- Companies who are in one of the primary B2B industries.*
- Companies whose offering has a unique and specific product differentiator.
- Companies who possess benefit to the potential customer.
- Companies with accolades and/or social proof.
- Companies with a specific market that you target.

NOTE: The primary industries are specific to SHP and they way it identifies major industries of its clients. Examples of these would be marketing, information technology, software, insurance, etc.

If you identify with any of these bullets, this method has been designed to provide the mindset, perspective, strategy, tools, and direction necessary for the foundations of cold call success.

RESULTS FOR THE MASSES

But how will a method work for you to achieve consistent cold call results?

The answer is a *conversation framework.*

A *conversation framework* is an organized order of talking checkpoints that are crafted to emulate a first interaction with a potential customer. It contains organized words, phrases, and questions we consider "strong bones," that enable cold callers to flesh out a structured and purposeful conversation with their own personality. We have found this transfers to a higher level of authenticity in delivery while never sacrificing the structure and purpose of what we are saying. The result? Leads and appointments for every cold caller and a method that works with results for the masses.

To peel back the layers, let's break down the idea of "strong bones" in a cold call conversation framework.

I have heard the following from salespeople over the years:

"Try this quick script I used to set an appointment last week," or, "use this line that has been working for me—I've set a few appointments using this quick bit of humor in the beginning of a cold call."

Sound familiar?

Here are a few more specific examples:

- "Hi [NAME], can I tell you a quick joke?"
- "Hi [NAME], do you have 24-and-a-half seconds for me to tell you why I called?"
- "Hi [NAME], how are you today? How have you been?"
- "Hi [NAME], you weren't expecting my call, and you might hate me for calling you out of the blue."

At best, these are the results of individual effort, personality, and testing; at worst, they're used by a few sales people as a dependent tactic and crutch. Before I share how The H2H Method™ is different, I want to make a disclaimer: these tactics are *just fine*. In fact, they're good, creative, and work in the right context.

In fact, I use them myself. Sometimes, when I've called to speak with a decision maker but am intercepted by a gatekeeper who asks what the call is regarding, I'll say sarcastically, "Yes. This is Ryan, I'm a sleazy salesperson trying to get a hold of [DECISION MAKER NAME]."

This type of opening technique—using a bit of dry humor and pausing to incite a reaction from the gatekeeper—is atypical to the cold calls they receive daily. According to Sandler, this type of "pattern interrupt" changes the momentum and direction of an otherwise rote cold call interaction.[2]

Pattern interrupts have helped me get through to decision makers and set appointments. However, you won't see much of this and other techniques in any part this book, because it is a unique characteristic of my own personality to say things on the phone in my own, innate style. Remember, *personality preferences* in a cold call are best chosen by *you*. A *conversation structure* is about strong bones. Your personality, humor, and commentary along the way add authenticity and candor to the structure of a conversation used by anyone. What works for you may not work for someone else. Test and refine your own preferences for comfortability on the call. Adding personality to the foundation provides a great selling experience to the prospect.

In the image, see the tree diagram. This represents the H2H Consultative Conversation Framework. The *preferential add-ons* are just a small part of a structure. What's different about The H2H Method™ and its depth is that it's meant for the masses and for the long term. New tricks and one-liners are trendy and fashionable, but much more fleeting than what serves our purpose here. While I've developed much of the original framework from my own calls, we have been boiling down, distilling, refining, improving, and delivering through iteration after iteration to build a script framework and cold call method capable of delivering results for the masses. We've worked diligently to truly define and live what "human-to-human" means. In other words, this isn't "Ryan-to-human" or "Traijhon-to-human" or "Cheryl-to-human." We operate by asking, "What is the person-to-person *conversation structure* that will convert cold calls at the highest rate possible for the largest set of sales development reps (SDRs) *and* personality types to the broadest markets?"

Gatekeeper

Preferential
Add-ons

Preferential
Add-ons

Quick Prop
(QP)

"Hi! How are you?"
"I understand you're busy."
"Is this a good time?"
"I didn't catch you at a bad time, did I?"

"Do you have a moment to speak?"
"I'll be upfront with you, this is a sales call."
"Do you have 26 seconds to hear why I
called?"

Hone-in
(Hi)

— Bridge Statement —

Calling Prop
(CP)

Discovery Questions

Extended Prop

Next Steps
(NXTS)

Qualifying Questions

THE
H2H
METHOD

H2H
SALES SCRIPTS
COLD PHONE CALLS

Handling
Objections

There are plenty of structures out there that work. However, the topic and studies have been largely left underdeveloped in the space. I've seen successful cold calling *conversation structures* outside of H2H work well, but the depth of content around how to implement effectively and consistently is largely unfound. As a result, I see many weak and unfollowed frameworks out there. For example, here is one I hear quite a bit on when I receive phone calls from cold callers:

1. Opener
2. Request for meeting
3. When confusion set in, double back on what the offering is
4. Pick out a meeting time
5. Hang up

I'm not going to say it never works, but the reliability of these steps for sustained cold call success with quality relationships built leaves much to be desired on a cold call. Prospects are left confused, verbally committed to something they aren't sure of, and with minimal thought provoking interactions to begin transferring belief in a new offering. This is what we hope to course correct and provide a structure for influential and belief transferring beginnings. Here is a simplified version of the tree diagram to show how a conversation structure can look with stronger bones:

1. (Opener optional) Intro
2. Opening Discovery Question
3. Tailored Value Prop
4. 2nd Discovery Question
5. (Optional) Additional Value
6. Next Step Identified and Agreed To
7. Housekeeping
8. Qualifying Questions Answered and Documented
9. End Call with Next Steps Confirmed

Defining and duplicating efforts with consistent results is the answer that helps us know if we've answered the question correctly. How can this be done? Well, for starters, it takes more than just one or two people. When I first developed the method, it was raw and unrefined, but there. It was converting a 2% to 4% appointment-setting rate (one sales appointment set in every 25 to 50 calls) on dials across multiple industries. The results were encouraging, but I knew my personal testimony wasn't enough. I needed to separate myself from the method and prove it would work for everyone. SHP would provide the case study for H2H.

Since then, SHP has gone from a group of three freelancers to a full-service business that serves 60 to 100 unique companies across the globe and makes between 40,000 and 75,000 outbound dials per month (at the time this book was written). This has given H2H a laboratory for constant refinement. Our client SDRs at SHP deserve immense credit for being open to learning and using this scripting framework and method to help identify a cold call conversation method that works in modern calling. Their work has been nothing less than illuminating for pinning a sample of the entire market as it relates to cold calling results and metrics. We have seen some cold call naturals adapt quickly. We have also seen some diamonds in the rough work very hard over a long period to slowly and ultimately see their appointment-setting rates bloom. Our diverse set of U.S.-based remote salespeople deploy The H2H Method™ at SHP on behalf of our clients. There is a tight process and a fast pace team members must subscribe to in order to succeed. Many client SDRs come to SHP with a natural talent for cold calling that enables them to adapt and have success with multiple campaigns quickly. Others struggle with a natural knack, but have the drive, work ethic, and openness to stick with it long enough to find success. Regardless of the SDR archetype, we see The H2H Method™ impacting their performance as it accelerates their impact as a foundation and tool for cold conversation success.

We've been collecting data over the past few years from our SDRs and have seen appointment-setting rates double from year to year. For example, see this quick chart on the same SDRs performance changes from Year 1 to Year 2 using the method while working at SHP:

Year	Dials	DM Convos on Dials %	% Change Convos	Appt Set on Dials %	% Change Appt Set on Dials	Appts Set on DM Convos %	% Change Appt Set on DM Convos
Year 1	50,130	9.21%		0.83%		8.99%	
Year 2	128,715	9.62%	4%	1.66%	101%	17.28%	92%

Note that not only did the number of raw dials double (some due to some starting at different parts of the year, and some because efficiency was increased), it also improved conversions by 92%. In other words, it wasn't just more conversations that contributed to the change, but it was also that these reps learned *what* to say (and not say) once they were on the phone with a decision maker.

While there are certainly more factors than "script" impacting performance—such as industries called, disparate products and services, tone of voice, pace of response, ability to overcome objections, and more—the fact remains that *each one of these SDRs was introduced to The H2H Method™ during initial onboarding and continued to learn the method in-depth through the next year.* Through daily role plays, further education on core components of calls, learning the *Superhuman Sales*™ Skills, and more, these SDRs increased their performance—not just in calling for one product or service to a select few target markets, but while calling for multiple products and services in a varied number of industries and company sizes.

Learning *the conversation connecting humans to value* was what drove these results forward in the end. The H2H Method™ for Cold Calls method was at the core of this transformation in results.

In this imperative and dynamic conversation that takes us from 0 to 1 in the sales process, *everything we do on the phone matters.* The goal of this book is to help you change the way you think about human-to-human phone sales call conversation structure—to improve your success rates in today's world.

ROADMAP (OUTLINE)

Before we go any deeper, I want to take a quick moment to run through the outline for the remainder of the book. We'll overview each section so you can prepare appropriately to dive into its content.

The way we've designed this is to first look at things from a high-level, philosophical/theoretical viewpoint, and then start to drill down further as we go. This way, by the time we get to the nitty-gritty details, you'll have some context as to why we're going about things the way we do.

Section 1 discusses the philosophy behind H2H. We'll cover:

- The what and why behind The H2H Method™.
- Some bad history of cold calling.
- Examples of what poor sales ethics look like today.
- What's missing from the art and science of cold calling.
- The new era for the craft of cold calling.

Section 2 covers some of the strategies we've honed, including:

- The 4 Elements of Cold Calling Success.
- The BRT and what it looks like before and after we meet someone when beginning a business relationship.
- The purpose of a cold phone call. This is probably the most fundamental and impactful part of Section 2. If we know the purpose of cold calling, then all of our other behaviors are derived from it.
- The Trust Umbrella: a visual depiction of the theoretical, strategic, and tactical parts of a cold call that need to align with trust.

Section 3 covers topics you might not be used to seeing in a sales book. If successful companies have a mission and vision statement, then why not a sales conversation methodology for the masses? Here, we explore *principles* of the method.

What does it mean to reinstate our mission as outbound sales-people using the phone to generate business? In this section, we'll discuss:

- Some of our values and the actual principles through which we deploy our skill set.
- Our value statement. You didn't think we were going to have a value statement, did you? This summarizes our values in a statement meant as a guideline for how we treat others when cold calling.
- Finally, some of the characteristics of a cold call. These are the behaviors of execution while speaking to a potential customer, cold.

Section 4 will cover script frameworks, examples, and our methods anatomy. Here are a few bullets about the section:

- We'll take a microscope to the cold phone call from a practical and tactical level using the 4CX4 component structure.
- We'll introduce and overview the 3 H2H cold call script frameworks
- We'll zoom in on things at a word-by-word level to learn the make up of every part of the conversation.
- We'll end this section with some examples of real scripts used to generate successful results in several industries.
- We'll wrap up the technical and tactical section with ancillary cold call topics such as gatekeepers, objections, and voicemails.

Lastly, Section 5 is our bookend to Trust Call. Closing out the book, we'll suggest an outlook on how to incessantly improve the quality of your calls and conversations and also take a stab at what the future may look like.

CHAPTER 2
WHAT IS THE H2H METHOD™ FOR COLD CALLING?

The H2H Method™ for Cold Calling has been built as a guardrail, for beginners to seasoned sales professionals, with the purpose of translating professional sales messaging into an easy-to-use conversation format for twenty-first-century sales conversations. The method is meant to maximize results without losing trust with prospects. H2H stands for human-to-human and reflects our belief and confidence that adding humanity into the sales & buying processes will help reverse the unseemly reputation it has gained over the years.

METHODOLOGY INTRODUCTION

The H2H Method™ for Cold Calling has been in development since late 2014. Digital marketing was growing rapidly at that time and was quickly becoming a staple for any viable business in the rising digital age. Forces were aligned against methods considered "old school" or "traditional"—those which relied on basic human communication skills such as person-to-person or voice-to-voice interaction.

The aversion to human communication in sales and marketing wasn't just because of the popularity and demand surrounding digital channels. There were other factors at play. First, years of scams, schemes, and inciting buyers' remorse in droves had given telemarketing and the sales profession as a whole a bad reputation. Salespeople utilized poor sales ethics to swindle and coerce potential buyers into trading their hard-earned money for empty promises and lies; many times, they embodied the pesky characteristics that appear whenever anyone ever mentions the word "telemarketer," or "used-car salesman." You have probably heard "cold calling is dead" or "the phone doesn't work" in modern business development strategy. These were attempts to drive the final nail in the coffin for an already battered and worn means of generating new business.

The methodology was meant to bring these traditional forms of communication back to sales and marketing—to give them a new meaning and reshape how alternate channels outside of strictly digital environments can enable small, mid-size, and enterprise-level companies alike. We believe these companies can take their destiny into their own hands by finding success in outbound, human-to-human marketing and sales practices that diffuse and shed old, poisonous methods of doing business while building back trust in the marketplace. We predict these methods will be more successful than we have thought possible in recent history. It has also been founded on years of testing. We've honed our skills to combat stigmas and hardened views within the marketplace and enable trust with potential buyers while offering and providing value when they likely would not have engaged otherwise. It has been refined, tested, and proven in dozens of industries, and it continues to develop. The marketplace's wants and needs consistently shape the method. We adapt to what we hear so what we do and say are in harmony. While this method has lessons that can be applied now, it is not finished. What we've created is the first of many chapters on how humans connect to value in the marketplace.

The H2H Method™ for Cold Calling has had a consistent strategy in all channels, whether it be a cold conversation over the phone, a gatekeeper conversation, email copy, a sales presentation or demo, a sales closing, or a variety of other sales conversation scenarios. The primary reason for creating the methodology is to provide definition in *striving for and maintaining the highest level of sales performance, while committing to a human approach that opposes the inducement of customer regret and buyer's remorse.* In other words, we aim to achieve the highest possible results without ever losing trust from potential customers.

The H2H selling mindset is derived from that overall objective. This is important to understand, as it helps position our mentality as one that seeks highest performing results possible while not engaging in activities that may endanger the relationship with the prospect we are selling to.

In fact, the mindset of H2H has many applications outside of The H2H Method™ for Cold Calling. Many environments requiring a high level of performance from people can glean greater levels of results from the objectives behind H2H. For example, coaching, sales management, and organizational leadership can use similar principles to achieve greater and more sustainable results for the long term. *H2H is a practice that pushes the limits of high-level results while sustaining relationships with people.* The creation of The H2H Method™ has emerged as a result of applications seen not only in H2H Sales Scripts® (our sales script products and services) but in the aforementioned examples. Stay tuned for more on The H2H Method™ as a more global organizational performance method applicable to almost limitless places where people and results are needed.

DEFINITIONS

Finally, placing a visual on what a method is helps label and organize how our learnings apply. Below is an umbrella image, or inverted foundational pyramid, with an overarching theme. The idea is that all actions need to align with the overarching philosophy. The method is the culmination of all layers cycled as a process.

To be crystal clear, let's look at the definitions of each and how they apply:

- **Philosophy**.

a.) Merriam-Webster defines philosophy as the most basic beliefs, concepts, and attitudes of an individual or group.[1]

b.) Oxford Languages defines philosophy as the study of the fundamental nature of knowledge, reality, and existence, especially when considered as an academic discipline.[2]

  - **Strategy**. A strategy is a plan of action or policy designed to achieve a major or overall aim.[3]
  - **Tactic**. A tactic is an individual action to complete towards the strategy.[4]
  - **Technique**. A technique is how a particular task is executed.[5]

A method then can be described as a process or system for accomplishing something.[6] We see these 4 layers as symbiotic and needing to be repeated to properly scale cold calling effectively. These words and concepts will be used throughout this book to flesh out the layers for best understanding and use.

CHAPTER 3
WHY THE H2H METHOD™ FOR COLD CALLING

THE
H2H
METH♥D

There are debates about sales scripts everywhere. Do you use them, or not? Do you say them word for word? Do you avoid them so you don't sound like a robot? What if the conversation goes off track?

All these questions are valid, so don't stop asking them. The problem with the idea of scripts isn't the science or the step-by-step rigamarole, it's the perception of disingenuous interaction with someone. That means when salespeople encounter a sales script for the first time, it can feel, well, less than personal. It doesn't feel like we are communicating as our true selves would—especially if we didn't write the script. On the other hand, there is certainly an art to sales conversations. In fact, top performers tirelessly rely on creative and unique ways to win next steps with prospects.

In sales, however, science comes before art.

For the vast majority of sales organizations, sales processes are scientific approaches meant to identify successful and measurable ways to convert sales. This allows sales leaders to see the math of projected goals *before* investing in the teams needed to achieve them. And this matters because when we have a goal in mind, we can create and establish repeatable paths to help us achieve those

27

goals at scale. If we think of sales scripts & conversation structures as a small sample of a repeatable sales process, we can see how using them at scale could help our entire team send a widespread message to the marketplace we are speaking to.

We see sales scripts for cold phone calls as *the* necessary tool for quickly converting at the highest levels. We have found scripts act as a guardrail in a blizzard of conversation. We have found if we cut through the noise, using a sales script helps expedite learning and deliverability of a succinct message when scaling with a team. It is also a documentable conversation that continues to sharpen over time. As the market changes, so does our language. Efficiency and effectiveness are multiplied when scripts are updated, allowing our team to pick up where we leave off as new members join. This cycle enables our micro-sales process within the bigger picture to improve efficacy and viability over time.

This is where science and art work together. Art in sales comes once the mechanics have been internalized. Once we understand the bones of the message and script, and have fully digested the reason for each part, creativity begins. If scripts are the building blocks of a bonafide message, then creativity can be utilized more freely once the mechanics and framework become second nature through repetition.

This doesn't mean scripts are only for beginners! Any time you start a new sales position, your current company launches a new product, or when you look to change your target, *the messaging has to change*. The words and phrases you use to resonate in the buyer's mind need to be thought through, identified, and learned by the salesperson making the call.

Whatever has happened, the act of cold calling has been one of the most dreaded activities within the spectrum of marketing and sales channels in recent history even though it has been around longer than many. But why? Salespeople and leaders find it difficult to cold call because they either don't have the time, don't know how, or simply . . . just hate it.

We don't blame them, really. And why should they need to cold call? Is anyone even picking up the phone? If digital marketing is working for them and bringing them leads—and cold calling is just an old-school, outdated, abrasive, and deceitful form of coercion—why would anyone gravitate towards it?

Because *humans still gravitate towards other humans*.

Look—digital works. It even gives buyers the most control. But what is lost is the speed of trust that can occur when humans speak in live conversation. This is why H2H is so relevant today. While potential buyers deal with unanswered questions, automation, spam, ads, click funnels, and scams, human-to-human, voice-to-voice interaction is seemingly at an all-time low.

If honest salespeople can understand the pain potential buyers have experienced from untrustworthy salespeople and the subconscious craving for live conversation, then cold phone calls can still be an even more impactful and effective way for moving from 0 to 1 in the sales process. It can provide prospects and be valuable to lives and businesses in the twenty-first century.

CHAPTER 4
THE BAD HISTORY OF COLD CALLING

T he H2H Method™ for Cold Phone Calls was born from a period of the telemarketing and boiler-room scams and schemes that scarred consumers and threatened the sales development industry from the 1970s through the early 2000s. This threat—combined with the rise of digital marketing and sales fueling the "cold calling is dead" movement—spawned a new channel for traditional advertising, exacerbating the stigma attached to the cold call outbound sales profession.

Currently, two main threats face outbound cold calling. The first sales threat, what I call "Modern Sales Failure," stems from *poor sales ethics* combined with a new, exacerbated reaction from potential buyers experiencing the *natural law of buyer resistance.* This exacerbation is what I call the *salesperson stigma.*

The second threat is the rise of digital marketing. Web design, SEO, Google Ads, and other digital inbound channels have tantalized inbound marketers and business owners to favor digital as a primary channel for new business opportunity. Its proliferation has created a platform to prove digital marketing's efficacy and denounce traditional outbound channels such as cold calling.

NOTE: There is a third potential threat: the advent of artificial intelligence and voice AI. Some companies will undoubtedly attempt to use this developing technology in their telemarketing and sales calls. At the time this book was written, there was no widely used voice AI capable of mimicking a human cold caller in live conversation with prospects successfully enough to permanently replace entire sales departments. While they're not a threat now, it is hard to predict exactly how sophisticated these bots might become. Could they evolve to hold enough conversation to build trust with prospects? Could they empathize or react with precise timing to objections? Could they set meaningful next steps? Could they ever build trust in themselves, the process, or the product? If they develop to this point, they could pose a threat to replacing cold callers in the future. Salespeople need to be aware of potential impacts to their industry—and ready to intentionally differentiate their skill set from their robotic counterparts.

It's no wonder digital marketing and sales gurus leveraged Modern Sales Failure while buyers were still building trust with internet transactions and eCommerce in the 2000s. Digital marketers knew buyers were sick of the same old sales tactics found in boiler rooms and telemarketing scams. They knew buyers wanted control and the ability to find what they needed when they needed it (and not when the salesperson wanted it). This makes complete sense–especially when the buyer's only other option was being swindled and hard-core closed by an aggressive, domineering sales person.

The good news? H2H exists to combat the noise and reimagine trust-building cold calling methods relevant for the twenty-first century regardless of the enemy faced. In short, real live human beings with trust-infused purpose can win the war against the cold call stigma.

CHAPTER 5
WHAT CLASSIC "POOR SALES ETHICS" LOOKS LIKE

Regardless of your background, if you are old enough to read this book, you've most likely received some type of scam phone call, been on the receiving end of a hard-core close, or have been presented with a lemon by a snake-oil salesperson. Many of us sense the phenomenon of poor sales ethics, but let's actually list what those things are so we aren't just speaking in platitudes.

What's ironic is the examples I will give may seem less common in the twenty-first century; but these classic, outdated, poor sales techniques are still used today, even if they look a little different than they did twenty years ago. I couldn't believe this was the case when I compiled my list for this section, but short-cuts, lies, and coercion are happening right before our eyes.

While I do believe many classic techniques and ethics are less present today than forty years ago, I think it's crucial to point out the worst of the worst so we can pin down and reject any of these examples as we continue to advance the sales profession in modern selling.

IRRELEVANT, POOR, OR FAULTY OFFERINGS

If your product or service isn't relevant, who are you truly help-ing? Even if you're using effective techniques, have a good process, and are building relationships, if the product behind the pitch isn't helping anyone, should you be offering it? That means no one will have a good experience, and the business will soon fail or need to quickly pivot.

For example, have you bought a black-and-white TV from Best Buy in the last thirty-plus years? No! At least I hope not. (If I have to say why I'm asking, I should probably write an entire additional book on product relevance.) If a TV business doesn't pivot soon and start selling to only antique stores or collectors who are looking for black-and-white TVs (okay, now I'm stretching to try and come up with something), then the market will quickly reject them.

It isn't malicious, of course, but that kind of failure speaks to the capacity of the company to be attuned to the market and how they can serve it. Businesses with poor or irrelevant offerings aren't going to last, anyway. With technology moving so quickly, software and digital products can quickly become irrelevant. This is why constantly listening to our customers is so important. Not only will we hear them and be able to speak to their needs, but we'll also be able to have an offering that is relevant and can actu-ally help them. Cold calling, by the way, is one of the only channels currently offering live feedback.

It's no wonder many of the most successful projects done at SHP fall in our "unique solutions" category, which we created to resemble new offerings to marketplaces. "Unique solutions" is our name for those offerings we work with that possess innovative qualities or first-to-market likeness. These tend to create curiosity in the prospect's mind and typically reflect an acute sense of an industry's wants or needs.

You've probably seen scam movies, like *Wolf of Wall Street* and *Boiler Room*, that are based on true stories about flawed sales people ripping off consumers and other types of buyers. Telemarketing scams have ruined the name of cold calling and it continues today. Just in October of 2019, a telemarketing ring was busted in Arizona for scamming seniors out of approximately $40 million.[1] The situation sounds all too familiar:

> *Police say the company made a variety of false promises in order to convince victims to provide their debit or credit card information over the phone. The victims were promised thousands of dollars in return as well as a 100% money-back guarantee, making it appear risk-free . . . The Federal Trade Commission partnered with the investigators, and approximately $7 million of the fraudulently obtained money was identified and recovered for return to the victims.*

> *The suspects involved have been arrested and charged with several felonies, including conspiracy to commit fraudulent schemes, money laundering, theft from a vulnerable adult, illegal control of an enterprise and unlawful telephone solicitation.*

This sad truth is yet another reason why the human-to-human method in sales and marketing is needed. Products and services that build trust back in the marketplace through quality, truth, and relevance can help reestablish connection and faith in potential buyers.

AGGRESSIVE SALES TECHNIQUES

A few years ago, I was referred by a connection to a sales executive on LinkedIn who wanted to sell me their software. I took a demo they asked to set up. After seeing the product, I liked it, but it wasn't something we were ready for. Interestingly, after the presentation our leadership team discussed the software for months. We still weren't ready to adopt it, but we were discussing it in the background. Some time passed. Eventually I heard back from the sales executive on LinkedIn. Here's how the conversation went down:

Sales Exec (11:46 am): "Ryan, you ready to do that test drive we discussed six months ago? Is now a better time?"

Me (11:48 am): "No, I'm not ready yet."

Sales Exec (11:48 am): "Sweet! I will let [referrer's name] know the intro was pointless. Good luck brother!"

I mean, damn! If I was in his shoes, I would have been frustrated too, but that was quite the backlash of a response. Did you notice that I included the timestamps? Based upon the rapidity of his response, I deduce his reaction was an emotional one. Oh, and by the way, he "disconnected" with me from LinkedIn after this.

Either way, this happened in 2019—rather far into the twenty-first century! The point? People still act like this! The definition of what it means to emphatically *not* be "human-to-human" is anchored in this type of exchange.

Remember, being human also means having grace and mercy with people. After all, no one is perfect. It's all about how we respond to another's actions. This person in the example didn't reconcile, but instead chose to lean into the damage in our sales relationship and, ultimately, broke trust with me. This was thought-provoking for me; it made me question what and where the boundaries are between defending ourselves and acting aggressively toward another person?

To be fair, most sales professionals come by these terrible tactics as a natural part of their sales training and education. Case in point: my first job out of college, with a home-remodeling company. While they serviced homes, they labeled themselves as a sales company (selling home remodeling). I was hired as a sales development manager, generating leads with potential customers so sales reps could go visit homes and sell their products. It was where I cut my teeth in sales.

I distinctly remember that the sales leader in our organization was a quintessential, cutthroat, hard-nosed, aggressive sales leader who radiated confidence but instilled fear in everyone below him. While I wasn't directly going to homes to sell the work, I was involved in the meetings the sales reps were in. We would crowd 200 or more sales people from all over the region into massive conference rooms for quarterly sales meetings. While leadership always covered a variety of topics, at some point the message became about doing whatever it took to get the sale from our homeowner customers.

And I mean anything. Sales reps shared stories about fellow reps who wouldn't leave a customer's home while trying to one-call-close a deal. Customers would tell the salespeople they weren't interested in signing and paying the first time they received a "free, no-obligation" estimate, and somehow this meant the sales rep would be triggered to dig their heels in even harder. Sometimes it even got so far as homeowners calling the cops on the salesperson in order to get them to leave the house. I remember after one of these instances, our sales leader inexplicably yet distinctly said, "God bless you" to salespeople who tried something so outrageous to get a sale. They didn't get the sale, of course, but they had proven to our manager they would fight to the death, so to speak, without any regard for our customers (or themselves, for that matter) in order to squeeze money out of them. This sounds more like gang initiation than selling.

There were dozens of stories like this, but I'll save many of them for another day. The goal of this book isn't to document all of the crazy sales and aggressive techniques, but to point them out enough to share how to combat them. More on these stories in the near future . . .

PROCESS KINKS

One-Call-Close Process Attempts. I am really surprised when I hear this is what people want when they ask me to write their custom cold call sales scripts in modern day selling. Regardless of industry, I will without a doubt receive requests to write up a "one-call-close" script, simply because that's what they want to happen. Unfortunately, the desired efficacy of this process is far from reality.

I don't just see it in script writing, but also those companies who would like us to call for them at SHP. Sometimes, we receive requests from customers who would like us to one-call-close a prospect from first cold call contact, straight to contract signed. In today's world, when adding the *salesperson stigma*—it's a sure way to make people feel uncomfortable and risk trust. Let me just clear this up to ensure it's out of your mind: *there is no such thing as a one-call close from a cold call in the twenty-first century.*

Why? The reason is simple: in modern selling, a rapid, one-call close leaves no room for trust to be built. In fact, It dispels it. Processes without trustworthy communication will lean more towards a forced seller-focused cycle. These hurt buyer relationships, as they are designed to create a process that quickly brings the buyer into a sale, allowing no time to build trust or to learn what the buyer wants or needs in a way they will not regret.

In the thousands of campaigns we've run at SHP, not one campaign strategy was executed on the premise that our reps would "one-call-close." If one-call-closing was ever possible at any point in history, resisting it is now so intrinsically webbed in the buying fabric of potential customers who put up their guard against such a sin, that it's virtually extinct. Whether a buyer in today's age has experienced it, or have heard horror stories from someone who experienced it in a past era, it's in the genes of potential customers to immediately shield themselves from this approach. It screams scam, theft, and swindler.

The remedy? To slow the buying process in the mind of the customer, which speeds up trust. In turn, this can increase the velocity of the selling cycle again.

False Process. One time at SHP, a liquor company contacted us with interest in using our cold call service. The goal was for our SDRs to call wine and spirit stores in a particular city in an effort to open up accounts to supply their new spirit. Sounds innocent right?

No.

Turns out, it wasn't.

The client requested our team to use ten different callers, to call each location one time each, and ask if their spirit was in stock. Then, our script was to read so that our team members would call the store clerk and ask if the drink had been stocked yet (even though the caller and the client knew it wasn't). The potential client effectively wanted us to create a false demand by asking the clerk if the brand was in, encouraging the owner to inquire about buying in bulk.

Wild.

This process displays the kind of deceit that would potentially hurt the targeted stores by pressuring them to buy something that actually wasn't in demand.

These misleading processes are sometimes hard to identify. If we aren't careful, we can believe the ends justifies the means. However, these are some of the very poor sales ethics that have hurt prospects in the past and can continue to do so today.

Gimmicks & Schemes: "The Vegas Package". Who offers an all-expenses-paid round trip to Vegas . . . just . . . because? No one but the companies trying to sell you timeshares in Vegas, of course! Sign up with them; all you have to do to claim your prize is drive to an office three states away and sit through a two-hour meeting! How harmful could it be? A few hours on a Sunday, some gas money, fast food, and you now have yourself a free vacation to Sin City! Well, did you know the two-hour meeting is penance and a long sales pitch on their timeshare? Did you know they know you think this just a quick meeting to get through in order to get their ticket to paradise, and they are going to use that any way they can?

You've heard of this gimmick. Also known as "bait and switch," the too-good-to-be true benefit is presented up front and is then changed once the potential buyer has sunk their teeth in. If you really read the fine print, nothing faulty was offered, but the way the Vegas package was presented wouldn't lead you to believe it was an honest offer. Still, the fine print is now salient, and the offer is actually different than it appears.

Not H2H.

CHAPTER 6
THE MISSING HISTORY OF COLD CALL METHODS AND STRUCTURES

Another reason for this book is to fill the gap from the sheer lack of comprehensive, full conversation-length, multi-industry proven cold call conversation structures used at scale. While there is a growing number of books and content on cold call openings, tips, objections, suggestions, mindsets, outlines, and more, this niche sales improvement industry lacks focus and experience in the knowledge of cold calling success across multiple sectors and industries.

I believe the reason for this lack of content comes from two barriers. The barrier is that skilled cold call content creators have a difficult time separating their individual successes with a scalable conversation structure built for others to use effectively (and often, it's not feasible anyway). They train others on the successes they had with one or even 5 products. They teach what worked for them and have their trainees rinse and repeat. This can work, but many times there isn't an opportunity for learners to absorb the vital moments that make a lasting and quality connection.

Too often, cold call experts are very focused on the meeting, using their humor, one-liners, and techniques to garner verbal commitments as early as possible. While these are certainly helpful and needed, they typically represent a personality type, trend, or fad within selling. This focus takes away from the value-packed opportunity in front of them that is oftentimes missed. For instance, at SHP, client SDRs have multiple checkpoints to properly pass the internal quality team review, so management and clients know the pain points, product or service value-added, type of meeting set, qualifying questions answered, and other aspects discussed on the call.

While the quality assurance requirements are high, they're based on empirical evidence of meaningful conversation that connects in a way resulting in a higher number of meetings actually showing up. Too many cold calls "set a meeting" without quality on the other end. If prospects are "convinced" to go to a meeting, they will hang up the phone regretful and resentful that they "allowed" the salesperson to take them that far. If prospects don't see a true reason to go to the next meeting, complying on the phone with a salesperson regardless of how nice, cordial, or polite they were can result in a "demo no-show." If prospects aren't provided value, a pain, interest, curiosity, or other points eliciting a belief that next steps are important, don't plan on them being at the "meeting" you set. Even in the perfect cold call, show rates are rarely, if ever 100%, so leaving something on the table for next-step commitment dilutes the efficacy of the craft.

The second barrier to the availability of full-blown methods and structure is the capacity for cold call content providers to give relevant recommendations based on the dynamics of disparate and changing industry nuances. As we've established, many cold call experts typically have experience in just a few industries prior to giving global advice, which means it's almost impossible for them to provide focused guidance on industry-specific cold calling, let alone to know when to adapt and how in changing industry-from and industry-to combinations (i.e., commercial insurance companies targeting trucking companies versus grocery wholesalers).

This is one of the many reasons I founded SHP (it's actually mostly why). From the standpoint of my own limited industry experience, I knew making a macro impact would require a different approach.

I started slowly, by A/B testing, documenting, and evolving the base script. The script structure got longer as I enhanced it with more checkpoints and components. It split into two primary structures, then three. Finally, documentation and cataloging scripts by industry began. With thousands of different scripts in total, each was similar but had its unique parts. The writing itself became more important, as well. How to break down words so they fit the product/service expert, the person calling, and the prospect being called was paramount.

Cold calling in and of itself can work in multiple ways, but unlocking the secrets of its ambiguity and disparity through revision to work at scale is just the beginning. Clearing this hurdle can only be done through a study of human psychology mixed with heavy experience and empirical cold call conversation and conversion data. I hope to begin the process of building workable scripts and structures that will help even the most novice of callers to have success. Fortunately, we are already seeing the results with our superhuman SDRs at SHP. The process will continue to develop and evolve toward perfection. This is just a glimpse of the development.

CHAPTER 7
A NEW ERA

W hen I was just starting in my sales profession, I experienced Modern Sales Failure and the rise of digital marketing simultaneously. *Is this really what sales is?* I wondered In the back of my mind. *Even though I enjoy the process and I have some natural skill in it, is this my fate? Am I doomed to be a sleazy salesperson using an outdated method of connecting buyers and sellers?*

The light in this dark place is that people are still people. Humans are still humans. This constant still exists today and will in the future. People are not bionic—half robot, half human. Humans have the ability to forgive, see things in a new way, let bygones be bygones, and most importantly for salespeople—passionately desire something they consider valuable.

Despite buyers' tendency to resist, this ever-present pursuit of value doesn't end. Every person is different, but we all want more for ourselves, our families, and our businesses. This buyer paradigm gives sales people an opportunity for redemption. The H2H Method™ for Cold Calling enables this redemption by defining and constructing a strategy relevant to the twenty-first-century salesperson who wants to heal wounds and overcome barriers that scarred buyers have been carrying around for years.

At my core, I *felt* the benefits of helping prospects. I enjoyed working with potential buyers through those first crucial selling stages, when I would walk them through how a product or service I was offering could really help them in the long term. Thankfully, I discovered a movement going on in the wider world, beyond my own thoughts and convictions, to advance the sales profession. Developments such as sales-professional bachelor's degrees, passionate and knowledgeable LinkedIn influencers, authors, communities, and organizations within the sales space supported the advancement of the profession. These movements invigorated me, proving there were others experiencing similar journeys.

The H2H Method™ for Cold Calling is simply a piece of this global movement to repurpose what it means to have trust-building and value-driven sales conversations in the twenty-first century. It is part of the universal drive to positively impact prospective buyers with the hope that the pendulum shift will enable sales professionals to be more successful in helping people see the benefits in new products and services they never had the opportunity to experience.

SECTION TWO
LET'S BE STRATEGISTS

If I were to ask you about the first gut reaction to having family dinner interrupted at 6 p.m. by a telemarketing call, what would it be?

Not an endorphin release?

Not pure joy?

Why not?

That's the problem.

Why is it we're screaming in our skin when we receive those telemarketing calls (at any time during the day, at this point) and not experiencing the same feeling that comes from searching on Amazon for the jawn you're going to add to your birthday list?

As cold callers, this is the type of feeling we need to try and elicit from prospects by the end of a cold call, but how do we get there?

Remember, the ultimate end of using The H2H Method™ is to achieve the highest-performing results possible while never losing the trust of our prospects. And that's the theme I want you to keep in mind throughout the rest of the book. This is the anchor for our strategy.

The strategies we'll cover give a theoretical basis for any tactical application through our calling efforts. The 4 Elements, The Business Relationship Timeline, Purpose of the Cold Phone Call, and the Trust Umbrella build guidelines around our execution.

CHAPTER 8
IGNITING THE 4 ELEMENTS OF COLD CALL SUCCESS

I f you remember anything from this strategic portion, remember this: *Think of mastering the management and execution of cold calling like a fire that needs to get bigger and bigger, rather than a house that needs to be built so you can set it and forget it.*

This fundamental perception of how cold calling works provides wisdom in how to view calling - and how to consistently improve it. Like a fire that needs to get bigger and bigger, it takes infinite work. It takes analysis, materials, realignment, reactivity, proactivity, and more. Sometimes there is an opposite perception about cold calling or outbound in general. Because inbound marketing can reflect a house that needs to be built, and once it is set to live in it only needs maintenance periodically. While this is certainly a strategy that can work based on the channel, cold calling can't be perceived this way to provide sustained results. Consistent and continuous work is needed. The better the process, the better position for higher results.

This segways us to the idea behind the 4 Elements of Cold Call Success. As seen in the image below, there are four elements that need work in order for success to be possible. The analogy is based in the Fire Tetrahedron in which four elements must be present for fire to occur. These are fuel, heat, oxygen, and a chemical chain reaction. Similarly, Product Relevance, Target Market Accuracy, Messaging Strength, and SDR Fit are necessary for success in cold calling.

Each element has a subject matter of its own. However, I recommend thinking of The 4 Elements in the order of Product Relevance, Target Market Accuracy, Messaging Strength, and SDR Fit. The 4 Elements need enough work within each to maintain and then build the fire. I'll introduce each to provide insight into what makes up each element.

CHAPTER 9
PRODUCT OR SERVICE RELEVANCE

P*roduct or Service Relevance* is the ability of the product or service to meet the current wants or needs of the prospect. This element is important because it can often be overlooked. Many times, we assume our offering is exactly what the market wants and feel we have found something as special as the invention of the iPhone. However, that's often not the case. In fact, it can be difficult for many businesses to find exactly what is unique and currently relevant. Product or service value refinement may need to be completed in order to find relevance in the market when cold calling. Sometimes, when we fire up the four elements, this element can be the weakest of them all, and its collapse can have a devastating impact on our efforts.

For instance, let's say Ray's Web Design has just opened up their doors. Ray, the owner, started the business because he has designed a few websites for his friends. He receives some compliments on his work, so he decides he wants to start offering website building as his business. He goes to the market by cold phone calling. Since his friends had businesses in two different industries, his value proposition is he can offer websites to any type of business to help them gain web exposure so they can grow. He begins cold calling all sorts of different businesses. He calls software companies, architecture firms, insurance companies, and more. He begins collecting feedback. To his surprise, everyone already has a website they are happy with! And further, most of the potential customers seem frustrated to even hear from another web design company!

The problem here is Ray's awareness of his product's relevance. Unfortunately, in today's world, every business has a website! While there was a time when Ray's services would have been very relevant, they no longer are in today's world, at least by any measure of comparison to the time before websites were first widely adopted. This isn't to say Ray doesn't have potential customers, isn't able to grow, or isn't viable. What it means is he may have to place extra pressure on the other three elements in order to find success. In essence, he is missing a helpful part of the cold call success equation, and it will be more difficult to find scaled success.

All is not lost for Ray's business. There are ways to take his offering and redefine it so it is relevant. This may take some additional work on product development, but it can certainly be done. For example, Ray could find a smaller niche industry to the marketplace, say, sports field complexes, and positioned his product to work specifically for them? Now, this could differentiate himself slightly from his competition and make his service appear more attractive.

In addition, what if he created a DBA for this business and called it "Ray's Sports Complex Web Design?" Now, given the name of his business and what he offers, he is positioned to specialize in this newer market, differentiating himself even further! Lastly, since web design has become a commodity in the last ten years, what if he offered an additional service of a web portal where teams and clubs could log into the website, pick times and dates for their rentals right on the website, and make initial deposits for their field rental?

At this point, we have totally recreated Ray's offering and have now positioned his business as very relevant to the market he is reaching out to. There is a much higher chance his web design company will be received as one that can help the sports complex rental business. With his product relevance now increased, it's then up to the remaining three element pillars to do their job!

CHAPTER 10
TARGET MARKET ACCURACY

T arget Market Accuracy then asks, "who exactly is it you want to speak with?" Is it just one person? Or are there stakeholders and influencers you can speak with if the main "decision maker" is not available? How quality is the data? It may seem obvious, but let's not forget a cold phone call is different from other mass communication channels, such as email or social media, in which you have the opportunity to speak to the masses with just one message. Cold calling is a *one-on-one opportunity*. When you're speaking with somebody, you can't be communicating with multiple people at the same time.

This is why learning who you can speak with *before* jumping onto these calls is so vital. It may not be just one person or title. For example, you can get in touch with someone at an organization, and while they might seem as though they aren't the person you want to speak with, doing some additional digging can help you learn if that person is actually a stakeholder or influencer who could be the tipping point in conversation. By learning about every person you speak with, whether it be a perceived gatekeeper, receptionist, lower-level staff member, manager, or other, you can document their stake in the use and decision-making power regarding the product or service you were calling about. Make use of every conversation and leave no stone unturned. If you do, cold calls will appear to be a waste, and the juice won't be worth the squeeze.

CHAPTER 11
MESSAGING STRENGTH

M essaging Strength determines how well the value of your offering will resonate in the mind of the prospect. From this perspective, a dynamite script is really a reflection of messaging capacity. We like to think of it in terms of baking a cake: the raw value you offer are the ingredients, the recipe is your messaging, and the script is the baked cake! Establishing some of your offering's benefits, features, and prospect pain points will act as ingredients in writing our scripts. When you construct these into word and phrase combos well, it provides a smooth delivery that enables a message to resonate the most with your prospects.

Once we get to the right people on a call, words and how we deliver them are all we really have. What we say, what we ask, and the manner in which we deliver are what converts and differentiates high-performance sellers from low-performers. The differentiation is what also renders messaging as a massive variable. The ability, knowledge, and delivery can change the dynamic of conversation from zero interest to closed deal. This is also one of the reasons I love selling.

Messaging Strength and Target Market Accuracy are the two primarily within the caller's control and which have the widest span of options to adjust for success. Even within these two elements, there are a multitude of micro adjustments cold callers need to make to ensure success. This comes with an incredible amount of feedback learned from calling. Unlike many other marketing channels, cold calling provides live market intelligence based on conversation feedback with potential customers. In other words, when you speak to targeted contacts on a call, you can ascertain incredible information about where these people and businesses stand. This includes several key pieces of information that help you determine multiple factors, such as the right individuals to speak with, interest, need, pain points, and responsiveness to what you are offering. All of this data enables you to sharply attune to the market and make proper adjustments every time you are on the phone. These things help better prepare you for the next call.

CHAPTER 12
SDR FIT

The final element is *SDR Fit*. At SHP, we have found *SDR Fit* an indicator of success. Best success can depend on a couple factors, including personality fit and a combination of the industry we are calling from and the industry we are calling to. For instance, more outspoken and gregarious personalities are sometimes better suited to interact with industries than those with more monotone or soft-spoken personalities.

Education level can make a difference, as well. When considering the concept of mirroring, those with advanced degrees and more specialized vocabulary can have a harder time influencing conversation with owners of small retail and service shops, such as vape stores and auto mechanics. On the other hand, those with more direct or plainspoken approach have an easier time speaking to these industries while finding it difficult speaking to senior level executives.

Humans on both the buyer and seller sides possess a wide range of personality types, backgrounds, accents, skillset, product knowledge expertise, emotional intelligence, and more, impacting measurement and success. This adds to the complexity of isolating unknowns and finding cold call success when combined with existing variables. Whether you are an SDR, account executive, sales manager, executive, or business owner, SDR Fit, the question still exists about best fit.

At the end of the day, you will never close one hundred percent of everything always. However, you will always learn something. Consistent testing, documenting, refining, and growth is what is so intriguing and fulfilling about sales. There will always be something you can learn from and grow into. The idea behind The 4 Elements is to view the entire scope of what can make cold calling work or fail. If one is weaker than the others, it does not mean the fire will go out. What it means is the other elements must carry the burden to uphold its efficacy, or, work needs to be done to cover for the weakest link. More to come on The 4 Elements, but burgeoning success needs to consider all elements under a microscope.

CHAPTER 13
THE BUSINESS RELATIONSHIP TIMELINE (BRT)

CONVERTING TIME SPENT TO SELLING TRUST EARNED

L et's begin with a basic definition of a cold phone call so there is no confusion. According to Merriam-Webster, a cold call is "a telephone call soliciting business made directly to a potential customer without prior contact or without a lead."[1] What separates a cold phone call from other forms of dials is the receiver doesn't expect the call, and they likely don't know the company making it. All of those "unknowns" can result in resistance to the call.

Make sense?

Okay. Then let's begin with where the heck a cold phone call is in the timeline of a business relationship. At the beginning, or prior to first contact from a salesperson, whether it be a sales-development rep or account executive, there is 0, or no business relationship yet. You don't know me, I don't know you. Complete strangers. It's quite a unique scenario. In fact, it's the only moment when there is no relationship at all. Cold calling then is the segway from -1 to .01 relationship. After a relationship is made, it can never be a cold call ever again. You only need to ever speak to someone and establish a relationship once, ever! That's it.

What is going through the mind of the prospect, then? Once the cold caller makes the dial, a potential buyer answers a phone call from a stranger. The instant your human buyer identifies in their mind this conversation might be a "sales call," flight or flight can kick in.

If a relationship hasn't started, then it's difficult for prospects to trust you, enacting the response. We call this phenomenon the *natural law of buyer's resistance*. This is when a prospect feels someone is trying to sell them something and they push back. The *natural law of buyer's resistance* is completely accepted and valid. We all have limited resources, so it's natural for prospective buyers to want to protect those resources (like money) and put up a defense against anyone who is seemingly trying to take those resources from them; or at least, making them feel this way.

At the moment resistance kicks in, sales professionals are already in a hole. We are underground, negative. This is why cold calling and outbound sales development as a whole can easily acquire a bad rap. Your potential human buyer already has their defenses up. Instinctively, the scarcity of resources (money) and the unlimited supply of products and services for purchase are at odds. How else can they feel? They don't know you, what your product or service is, or what type of crazy tactic you might try to pull to take away a resource they use to survive.

This paints a dark picture of outbound cold calling, prospecting, and sales development as a profession. Add a sprinkle of *poor sales ethics* and a dash of *salesperson stigma,* and you have a cauldron simmering with a hot mix of "dirty jobs" written all over that recipe. Here is a graphic depicting the beginning of a sales, or, business relationship:

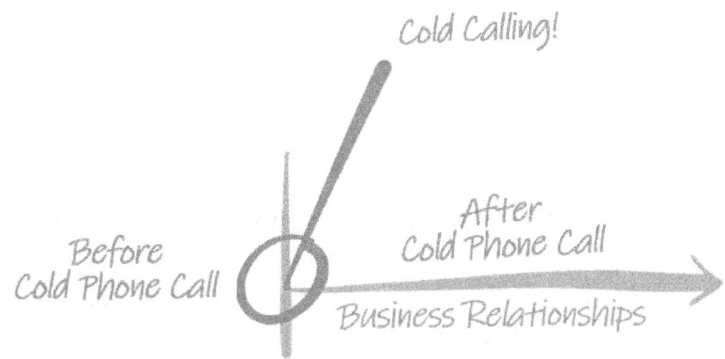

If you look at the sketch here, you'll see there is a vertical line intersecting and also establishing where business relationships begin. Everything to the left of this line is cold calling. We wonder why there is so much clash and aversion between prospects and salespeople in the beginning. There are many more "nos" than "yeses," and this is because the relationship hasn't started yet.

Cold calling is made even more difficult by the number of other marketing channels available. There are cold callers, of course, but there's also digital content, ads, banners, commercials, email marketing campaigns, contact marketing, and a variety of others enticing prospects to spend their very scarce resources. It's exactly how the marketplace works, and coincidentally makes things more difficult for cold callers. It is completely normal for potential buyers to experience the *natural law of buyer's resistance*, though, considering all the attempts from companies using different channels of marketing and sales in order to exchange those resources. But it puts added pressure on cold calling as a channel and makes it one of the hardest relationships to start. There are already so many forces against salespeople and the one-on-one encounter with their prospects' resistance.

APPLICATION

Back to The Business Relationship Timeline (BRT). Now that we have a little history and education about why a cold call is so hard, let's try to crack the code, so we have the gumption to actually make those calls! Within the context of this history, and with the *salesperson's stigma* in mind, we are trying to figure out how to start a relationship from 0 relationship to a minimum level of an established relationship we'll call "1". If you look back at the BRT sketch image, you see cold calling is before the intersection of "0" and "1" in a business relationship. A lot of times, it can feel like we're actually in the negative. Since we are trying to get from nothing to something, there is far more energy in the act, a higher perceived risk, and a wider range of possibilities in any potential response from the person we are trying to begin a business relationship with.

But once you break through the first conversation positively, it gets a lot easier, doesn't it? Once you have that initial conversation, you then have another. Maybe the next time it's a demo, discovery call, or in-person visit.

After this first meeting, the prospect begins to see the value. They begin to trust you, your process, and/or the product more. After this stage, it's a proposal, and then finally, a sale. They begin to use your product, adapting it to their own life and business process. The relationship doesn't stop here, either, and it is forever changed now that we can't go back to not knowing each other. A little later, there's the account renewal. You're on a first-name basis and you know each other's kids' birthdays, favorite bands, or sports teams. The farther you go on, the easier it is to continue that relationship at any level, since you got past that very first crucial point. The prospect's life has now changed because of this first call. Not only do they have the new product or service benefiting their business or life, now the prospect has a new relationship and connection they wouldn't have if it wasn't for that cold call. Since many cold calls start with awareness and move towards belief transference, prospects benefit additionally from the truth brought to them by the salesperson calling. Cold calling is a true win/win if done well, as hard as it may start for both sides in the beginning.

CHAPTER 14
PURPOSE OF THE COLD PHONE CALL

T he opportunity we have to rectify the name of sales, no matter how bad, is based on one of the fundamental natural laws of the buyer-seller relationship: trust. Trust is the catalyst in changing how we speak to other humans when connecting buyers to value.

This is exactly what will give you and your business an edge. If you are able to first master the conversation connecting people to value, much of your conversations after the initial call will come with ease!

If we speak to humans as they are, understanding what's important to them, we can provide an experience that builds trust again faster than any other source, all other things being equal. That's what this book is about. The human-to-human sales conversation is unlike any other, because it can break through the strongest barriers of the salesperson stigma and penetrate the shell buyers have formed after being scarred countless times. In sales, trust is everything. If you don't have trust, you don't have much. Here are the ways trust must be established before anything else can be done:

- Trust in the efficacy of the product or service being offered.
- Trust in the salesperson and/or brand.
- Trust in tactics and process.

Trust must come first in sales; otherwise, it is difficult to make things happen. This is especially true for outbound sales development—in first contact, cold introductions, and cold calls. There is so much negativity and stigma built up against outbound callers, we must establish a new mission in our calls. It can't be for lesser reasons. It can't be to hypnotize, charm, or distract. If it is, prospects are smart and will catch on quickly, dropping you from the call faster than you can say "ringtone."

Let's look at each of the three ways trust can or cannot be built, starting with *product* or *service*. As salespeople, we assume our product or service is what prospects want. If we're a salesperson working for a company, we look at the product's features and benefits. Then we go out into the marketplace, try to build value, and sell prospects based on what we have, assuming it's relevant or acceptable to the marketplace. But sometimes that's not the case.

In 2023, if I called you to offer your company a discount on the bulk purchase of Motorola Razrs from the year 2000 for your field staff to communicate with, how would you feel about the relevance and trust in my offer in today's high-tech, app-driven world? I hope you would say it's not good. With smartphones from Apple to Android processing faster than some of our home computers, the relevance of these flip phones in 2023 couldn't be farther from us.

On the other hand, some products are trusted to be very quality and relevant. There are droves of new software that make things easier and faster for companies right now. There are new, innovative physical products introduced to the market that are flying off the retail shelves or being used in manufacturing. There are also plenty of services providing time and cost savings while improving the state of the client's business.

In the context of cold calling, product and service trust isn't just about quality, but about the timing of macro product/market fit. Buying businesses need to be able to see the value add quickly, whatever the product or service may provide. In our example, Motorola Razrs may be quality and in working order, but in the fast-paced world of mobile telecommunications technology today, the ability to trust these devices will offer the best features and benefits available compared to the rest of the market in 2023 and beyond is at an all-time low. Said simply: Trust in the product or service is trust in real-time product/market fit.

Regardless of the relevant (or not relevant) product or service you're selling, you must build trust as a *salesperson*. We're going to talk more about this when we get to the section containing the sales values and H2H characteristics, but as a salesperson on a cold phone call, you *must* build trust on a personal level with your prospect.

The relationship really is between your prospect and you, so the way you conduct your sales activities has to build trust as well. Sometimes, that can be difficult. A salesperson often has to walk a fine line in order to achieve the maximum results possible while still keeping trust with prospects.

The fine line is something we'll cover, but being assertive and not aggressive, encouraging and not pushy, are example character-istics on the line between keeping and breaking trust. An example of a non-trustworthy salesperson is one who gets on the phone with a prospect and says they were forwarded to the decision maker when they weren't actually forwarded (this is also known as lying). Holding high values as a sales professional is the way we build trust. Prospects are going to test you. They want to test your character so they can catch scams when they happen (remember, *poor sales ethics*). We have to learn and adapt these principles, so when we get into those situations, we'll be on the right side of our prospect's favor.

Lastly is the capacity to build trust in our *sales process*, if we are going to win our prospects over. If we assume prospects feel resis-tance to salespeople, then slowing down the buying process in their mind is how we can build trust in our *sales process*. Losing this trust can happen a lot quicker than we think sometimes if we aren't careful in our process. For example, a pervasive issue in the home remodeling industry is the concept of a "free, in-home no-obligation estimate" for a consultation and proposal. It's a fine offer when pitched, but turns to an untrustworthy process when the salesperson is in the home, offers the price, and attempts to not leave the house until the homeowner signs the deal after multiple "no's" and requests for the salesperson to leave from the customer. Offering something as "no obligation" isn't a right of passage to abuse the word by acting aggressive and pushy. This type of process feeds the *salesperson stigma* and creates even more barriers between sellers and buyers.

When sales processes are in action, they communicate a step or objective for our prospects to follow. There is something ironic about trustworthy sales processes though. While companies may create sales processes for their organization to close the sale, much of a trustworthy sales process is designed around the buying behaviors of the prospect in an industry. A seller-buyer relation-ship, then, is quite symbiotic, requiring both the goals, objectives, and values of the offering from the seller, combined with the needs, acceptance, and decisions of the buyer. Since both relation-ships are needed for a sale, the selling party needs to pay close attention to the buying behaviors to create, build, and solidify the relationship.

CHAPTER 15
TRUST UMBRELLA

W hy trust though? While not arbitrary, it's also not the easiest to explain. I have asked groups what the purpose of a cold call is, and in response have heard them say something else (communication, value, interest, etc.). These steps are certainly part of it, but they don't belong here in the beginning, or necessarily in the fabric of everything we do.

Philosophically, there are three layers in a prospecting conversation, each of which are unpacked at different points within its execution. We've developed our Trust Umbrella to illustrate how each function of a cold call relates to the others.

The first layer is the relational, philosophical, or even spiritual layer answering the question of a cold phone sales conversation's purpose. This is trust. We've said before everything else we do as a sales professional from here forward must involve trust. This may seem limiting or restricting to the freedom and creativity within a cold sales conversation; however it does just the opposite.

Three layers make up the skeleton of the trust umbrella: trust is the overall goal or purpose, primary and specific objectives or strategies of the call come next, and then the tactics of the conversation we're in and the purpose of each one form the base.

Let's dig a little bit deeper to understand each layer a bit more.

Here in our trust umbrella is a visualization of those three layers and how they play out in a conversation. I cannot emphasize enough that regardless of what we're doing and what we're saying, *we have to build trust*. Every word we say has to be scrutinized and analyzed so everything builds in the right direction: towards the highest chance of converting a prospect.

Take a look at the umbrella visualization. At the top is our overarching theme to build trust. Underneath, we have the three strategies of a cold call or the three objectives. Those are *spark interest, diffuse the salesperson stigma,* and *sell the next step.* Last, we have the 4CX4. These are the tactical components of a cold call allowing us to 1) understand where we are within each part of the conversation, and 2) anticipate how to flex and move these around based upon the target we're speaking to.

SPARK INTEREST

Let's look at each one a little bit more, starting with the three strategies of a cold call. The first is spark interest. We must identify prospect pains or ways their business life is worse without your offering and then deliver features and benefits that make an impact and resonate with your prospect the most.

DIFFUSE THE SALESPERSON STIGMA

This one is probably the most relevant to what we've been talking about so far, because it has to do with diffusing and dispelling the *poor sales ethics* of a past era that have been transferred to you by prospects, even though they don't know you.

This can come in many different forms, but a lot of common places the *salesperson stigma* shows its face is through objections.

"Oh, no, I don't have the money right now."

"This isn't a good time for me."

"Is this a sales call?"

"What's the call regarding?"

"Does he/she know why you're calling?"

"Where are you calling from? What's your address?"

"What's your website?"

"I'm busy"

"(Click!)"

In these situations, it's best to respond with something that helps to diffuse the situation and build back trust. For instance, I might respond to the "is this a sales call?" objection with something such as, "Yes it is! I would love your partnership one day, but I understand there is a lot that we have to go through in order to get to that point. Really, the whole point of my call is to help you learn and see if this is something that could work for you if and when you're ready."

By eliminating some of the urgency they're feeling, even though you're not intentional about it, we're able to diffuse the *salesperson stigma* in those moments and sell the next step.

SELL THE NEXT STEP

As we've stated, there's no such thing as a one-call close in the twenty-first century from a cold call. So we have to identify what the next possible steps are. At SHP, we have different grades of interest based upon some basic rules we've established. It works by defining the "play-by-play" permission the prospect would be open to giving us at the end of the call. This is not only to meet prospects where they are, but also for internal measurement and benchmarking. For instance, is it just an email they're open to with no permission to call back? Are they open to a follow-up call, but maybe just not a specific date or time? And does a sales appointment, demo, or presentation at a specific date and time make sense as a next step as a result of the call? Identifying these play-by-play results not only helps you measure outcomes, but it also gives you options for building trust at the speed chosen by the prospect. By design, these stages of prospect choice have much of the "H2H" essence in them as well. Meeting prospects where they are while simultaneously moving them towards our sales goals at a measured pace is exactly the symbiotic movement we seek of a healthy seller-buyer dynamic.

THE 4CX4

The 4CX4 is the framework in which we entitle stages of a conversation in real time. By breaking up different parts of the conversation, we know what we are trying to accomplish in these specific stages of the dialog. What's unique about the 4CX4 is it can be fluid depending on the market we're calling into and what the conversation requires. The format it's in, as you see it in the umbrella, is our default framework, which is called the Consultative Conversation Framework (CCF). It looks like this: QP (Quick Prop), Hi (Hone-in), CP (Calling Prop) and NXTS (Next Steps). We will go into detail later in the book, but the ensuing explanations are a quick primer to prepare you for what's to come.

The Quick Prop (QP) is a quick statement or description of what you do to get the prospect in the right frame of mind and list a light benefit or feature as appropriate. The Hone-in (Hi) is a question that's designed to discover the prospect's familiarity with the product or service we're calling about and to encourage a conversation. Third is the Calling Prop (CP). The CP is the meat and potatoes of our call because it is our moment to instill belief in what we do by speaking on our offering's value. (We're going to be talking about The Value Proposition Trifecta later, which is usually delivered during the CP, and really helps us to scientifically define our value proposition as it relates to a cold call. This helps the value resonate the most in the mind of the prospect.)

And lastly, Next Steps (NXTS). The NXTS helps the sales process mark clear objectives for the salesperson and the prospect after that first call. While the NXTS objectives need to be cognizant of and sensitive to buying cycles based on the market, NXTS establishes what will happen after the first phone call.

The most impactful learning we gain from The Trust Umbrella is it provides us with just about all the topics we need to cover in the practical delivery of a cold phone call within The H2H Method™. The purpose of building trust casts a net covering everything underneath and provides checks for the words, phrases, tone, and delivery throughout our conversations. Keeping The Trust Umbrella close acts as a guardrail when we face unknowns, new conversations, and uncovered challenges in our cold phone calls.

CHAPTER 16
A STRATEGY SESSION

While we have identified trust as a primary purpose within the world of cold phone calling, there are tangible objectives that need to be met to experience success. Relationships and philosophical purposes are great, but without any practical application, no one knows how to apply something so abstract in a conversational format.

Former Chinese military general Sun Tzo once said, "Strategy without tactics is the slowest route to victory. Tactics without strategy is the noise before defeat."[1] Strategy gives us the path to reach our purpose—and that includes creating tactics that allow us to take small steps to meet our larger goals move things forward.

After writing scripts for thousands of companies worldwide and executing even more sales development phone prospecting campaigns with SHP, we've discovered three primary objectives that make for the most successful outbound call efforts:

1. Spark interest
2. Sell the next step, not the product or service
3. Diffuse the salesperson stigma

SPARK INTEREST

Sparking interest manifests itself in a few different ways within the cold call phone conversation. Here are a few ways sparking interest is a significant part of the cold phone conversation:

1. Sparking interest in the product or service
2. Sparking interest in how you can help the prospects, specifically
3. Sparking interest in you by building rapport in your prospecting
4. Sparking interest by having a sales conversation rather than a pitch session
5. Sparking interest in the brand

Let's dive deeper and explore these areas.

Sparking interest is primarily about generating awareness, desire, and need in the product or service we offer. Sparking interest, like other parts of the script, are pervasive and arise along different points of the conversation.

Sparking interest isn't just about delivering features and benefits surrounding the product or service knowledge. In fact, a majority of the words in our H2H conversations scripts *aren't* about the product or service. We find it more important to build rapport, identify needs, listen, and help to identify next steps. In other words, by having a sales conversation and not a pitch session, you are *actually talking with them like a human being*. You speak, they listen. They speak, you listen. It's no different in sales. While there is purpose and intent in your call, the only way to influence, persuade, and be a change agent at the highest level is by asking questions, talking, and listening to dialogue.

Finally, we are generating interest in our brand, our company, and our business. While this can be a longer play depending on how big or small your brand is, the way you hold yourself will reflect your brand. While there may or may not be much conversation about your brand in an initial cold phone call, the interest in your brand will develop after you have successfully sparked interest in your product or service, how you can both help them.

SELL THE NEXT STEP, NOT THE PRODUCT OR SERVICE

Many who have begun their journey with cold calling as a part of their sales development strategy have had a much different understanding of how cold calls work in real life versus when they first started. At SHP, we have had to advise many businesses looking to use our service that they should not ask for a sale or even something as small as a closed web registration for an event on the first call with a prospect.

Think about this strategy for a second. *Sell the next step, not the product or service.* What is it telling you? Building trust is in the slowing of the sales process. While it's counterintuitive, slowing down the sales process in the mind of the prospect can actually speed up trust with you, your brand, your product, and your process faster. Understanding the *salesperson stigma* will help speed trust in other ways, but understanding how to design a sales conversation around a sensible goal is paramount to converting at the highest levels while increasing trust with your prospects.

In the tactical approach section, we'll break this down at a practical level so we know exactly how it plays out in a cold call conversation format. For now, it's helpful to acknowledge that many times, the objective to identify next steps reveals itself when you take the time to analyze what would make sense for the particular market targeted. The most common one is some type of sales appointment: whether it be a quick 15-minute phone call, a 20-minute video conference call, or a 30-minute in-person meeting, a committed date and time to discuss and provide value is the baseline request. The *next step* doesn't always have to be a meeting though. Depending on your industry, it could be a webinar registration link, permission to send educational information, or even a follow-up call in a general time period down the road. When first forming a sales development strategy, understanding your marketplace and how the industry might respond is vital to the success of your efforts.

Remember our metaphor from Jim Collins: fire bullets, then cannonballs. Test your process at the beginning while learning curves are typically high. Then, home in on your target. Specifically, test what gives you the highest level of effectiveness for your time. At SHP we have found an appointment isn't always the best use of time because many decision makers can be too busy to commit. However, permission to follow up within a period of time is often readily accepted by decision makers because it doesn't commit them to something they cannot fulfill.

DIFFUSE THE SALESPERSON STIGMA

As a part of cold calling's bad history, the salesperson stigma rears its ugly head rather often in twenty-first-century sales conversations. Due to Modern Sales Failure, *poor sales ethics* mixed with the *natural law of buyer resistance,* remember, there is an uncanny aversion to sales calls and salespeople, as a whole.

Diffusing the salesperson stigma is a ubiquitous strategy for breaking down barriers and rebuilding trust in an initial call. This manifests itself in quite a few ways throughout the conversation. While the design of the conversation as a whole naturally diffuses the stigma, as does selling the next step rather than selling the product or services, it's also important to acknowledge that the responses or objections that typically come up in a call have less to do with a product in question and more to do with pressure the prospect feels. Many times, they feel they need to commit now and/or fear they are being pushed into something that they'll regret.

Here's an example of an objection or concern we've heard over and over when performing thousands of prospecting calls (and how to properly overcome the salesperson stigma):

Prospect: "You know, this won't work, we don't have the money for anything like that right now."

SDR: "Oh no worries! Yeah, that wasn't the point of my call anyway. We aren't trying to close any deals or sign any contracts right now. I was actually just calling to see if we can help you discover if this would make any sense down the road when you are ready and provide any help to you along the way."

In this objection, we see the prospect feels the pressure of being sold by the way they brought up money so quickly. The SDR's job in response is not to rationalize cost or push the product, as doing either of these would, but diffuse the pressure on the sale by reframing the point of the conversation. By resetting the course to education and fit for when the time is right, now a "NXTS" (appointment) may not be so bad.

———

If you remember anything from reading this entire book, remember this:

We don't mind if our prospect knows our conversation is a sales call, we just don't want them to feel like it is.

This is how sales conversations are flipped on their head. The moment they begin to feel it, we acknowledge it and begin to diffuse it. I have said this over and over to my consulting clients and to my clients at SHP. The moment the prospect *feels* like they are on a sales call, the slope can get very slippery. Work on identifying these moments.

SECTION THREE
PRINCIPLES

UNLEARN AND REFRESH

CHAPTER 17
RESTATING OUR MISSION

I realize we haven't uncovered too much of the technical, word-for-word scripts yet. Please hold on! Before I share the practical steps of the method, we must unlearn and refresh how we even angle our mindset on cold phone calls it's taken this whole book so far to unpack! Hang with me. We are getting close to the conversation tactics, language use, and scripts you need to get back to calling and converting! However, philosophy, values, and characteristics have virtually *never* been covered in cold call education and training. Slowing us down now will help us speed up our success later.

Unlearn and *refresh* are the key words of this section. If your sales method has a weak or soft foundation, there will always be cracks in execution. There will be deals lost, relationships damaged, and work to be done to fill in the losses. The difference with H2H is not just the success won using the method, but a foundation resting deep to bear the weight of the heights reaching the clouds and all that threatens the core.

Holding sales values that build trust is not an easy process to adopt. Often it can feel as though we are moving in slow motion, because we are making moves to slow the sales process. This can seem counterintuitive, as we have goals to meet with deadlines.

But as we've mentioned, slowing the sales process has the capacity to speed up the trust with prospects—and many times, it does. Sales values can cover and hold ground for the long term, so any potential customer will always be within reach, if they are willing to participate. If we build a foundation without principles, the inevitable crutch is to stop short these values and fall back to short-cuts and behavior leaving prospects feeling jaded, regretful, or hurt. Learning these values and principles before we go back to calling techniques and tactics give us a new, fresh perspective on how to conduct these super important conversations from 0 to 1 in the sales process.

I'm excited to share this section with you. Discovering these truths came from facing some ugly realities about sales in my career. I've experienced *poor sales ethics* in my career, both by practicing them and being sold to by others using them, and I couldn't continue my career in the profession without committing to something greater in how I would bring value to people. Restating our mission helps us unlearn what we've been taught and gives credence to reshape our mind and have an impact for positive change in twenty-first-century sales relationships.

CHAPTER 18
HUMAN 2 HUMAN
SALES VALUES

S elling values are specific descriptors of our selling behavior that clarify the meaning of each action we take. Because of those *poor sales ethics* of yesteryear, it's imperative to redefine what high-performing behaviors look like while maintaining trust with potential customers.

Truth and honesty are (I hope) common sense in this picture, but there is also a line of action we must define and not cross in selling situations. After all, we as salespeople are encouraging prospects to willingly give us their money in exchange for goods or services. It is too easy for poor, unethical sales practices to propogate and become common practice in sales organizations. This is why defining specific values to sell by and ensuring any action we take within our creative license in selling holds to a system in how to treat prospects.

In other words, a value statement helps us operate within a framework, while individual selling values help us to define the line between "good and evil" sales practices.

Consider the line between *poor sales ethics* and best practice. It's an area we don't often discuss, because the line between poor ethics and best practice isn't always clear . . . and so we fossilize.

But take heart: defining each area to the best of our knowledge sets the ground rules and gives us freedom to move.

Below are some of the selling values. It is not the *complete* list, by any means, or even the final definitions of each. Perfection is always a pursuit, so the focus should be on continuously finding new lines, making them clearer, and practicing execution of each within our abilities.

SLOW THE PROCESS, SPEED THE TRUST

Slowing the buying process in the mind of the potential buyer accelerates their trust. If that seems counterintuitive, consider what happens if we switch the words to say "speed the process, slow the trust." Isn't that statement reminiscent of the *poor sales ethics* we're all too familiar with?

While we've covered the *one-call-close* and its extinction, resulting in a slower process, a more current and relevant example to our everyday sales conversations is through common objections we all hear and face. While most sales professionals aren't diving into a conversation expecting to close a deal that day, many potential customers can "feel" the sales call in the conversation and immediately push back. This *natural law of buyers resistance* is a defense mechanism to protect their scarce resources. An objection we all hear and face after the sales professional asks for a sales appointment in a cold call is "I'm not ready to buy anything right now." This is a natural reaction and speaks to the pressure a prospect feels when they haven't yet developed the trust in the process to confidently proceed. While this may be true, the sales pro has the opportunity to turn this potential issue into a positive by resetting the expectation. Responding with assurance that the point of the sales appointment is simply to help them learn, provide value, and be a resource can slow the sales process in the mind of the prospect, giving them a bit of peace and ease around the process. By slowing the buying process down in their mind, it can build trust with the sales person and process much more quickly.

ASSERTIVE, NOT AGGRESSIVE

Assertiveness is communication in a timely, empathetic, yet tenacious manner that eliminates stigmatic reactions from prospects while never losing the relationship with them. It's the way we engage with prospects directly and proactively when there is a gap to fill, objection to handle, or belief to instill. For instance, let's say we reach a gatekeeper and are looking to get through to a specific name on our list. Assertiveness would be respectfully, yet with purpose and pace, asking for the person's name we're looking for. If the gatekeeper objects, we speak directly to them about what we do and our intentions. We don't sugarcoat, and we don't overpower by bashing the door down to get to our person.

If we're strong-arming our gatekeepers or prospects and overpowering them during the call, this can move us away from building trust by forcing prospects against the grain. In addition, aggressive sales behavior reflects even more *poor sales ethics*, contributing to the epidemic of the *salesperson stigma*. Another example of aggressive behavior could be cutting off your prospects in the middle of a conversation to get that word in about what you can do for them.

In the defense of the salesperson who is expected to produce results and reach goals, sometimes the line between assertive and aggressive can be difficult to know. Acting bashful or consistently cowering on a call can lead to no results extremely fast, but sales folks who cross the line to "convincing" can render prospects uneasy. The salesperson will find themselves listening to a dial tone or even winning deals customers later regret.

When our jobs depend on results, proactivity and assertion are required for survival (let alone success). Good faith effort is the key to finding the line within your own space. For instance, at the gap between the CP and NXTS towards the end of a cold call conversation, there is an opportunity to set an appointment with a prospect. It is the salesperson's job to move the conversation to an achieved NXTS. In some circumstances, the prospect may make noises or say things that suggest they would like to end the call. But if the

SDR notices this and is assertive as trained, the SDR may say to the prospect "Erin, before you go, the reason for my call is to see if you'd be open to having a quick 20 minute demo tomorrow on Google Meet. Would you be open to that conversation?"

An aggressive salesman might say something like, "Look, I've already spent 15 minutes explaining to you how this is going to work, twice. How about you give me my 15 minutes back tomorrow for a 20 minute demo?" Or, "If you don't accept this invite, it's going to make me look like an idiot in front of my boss. You aren't going to let that happen, are you?"

Assertive, not aggressive is finding a balance between proactively moving prospects along our sales cycle and following prospects down their buying cycle timeline until they are ready for our next steps without making them feel fear if they don't or feel they may regret the decision.

ENCOURAGING, NOT PUSHY

A very close value to Assertive, Not Aggressive is to be Encouraging, Not Pushy. Outbound sales is an influence-driven, belief-altering, evangelistic sales philosophy. Our job is to find pain, speak to it, be valuable, and change prospects' minds so they'll buy. You'll lose in outbound sales otherwise. However, drawing the line in the sand between encouraging and pushy means holding the belief that as sales professionals, we need to support the offering we are selling in a way that encourages our prospects to see its value without being pushed over the edge into doing so. But what is the difference there? When do we know we've crossed the line to pushy, seemingly forceful, or overbearing? Sometimes, the line isn't always clear and can differ from person to person.

This can come up at the end of cold call conversations. When both the cold caller and prospect have been through the entire conversation, the ending can be tricky. The cold caller is looking to identify and close the next step, while the prospect feels they have been patient, learned a thing or two, but are ready to get off the phone. The line between encouraging and pushy is often found here. Pushy could be asking for a commitment to meet after the prospect has given a "no" multiple times, while encouraging could be suggesting reasons for a next step that help the prospect while the prospect is unsure and before they provide a clear "no."

For instance, when we train our appointment setters to ask for the next step, we tell them the first "no" from a prospect after asking for an appointment is typically an emotional response, and they are to work their way back to asking a second time. We rarely see or hear poor reactions from prospects at this juncture. While some may feel they have already stated their position, one more request doesn't generally result in hangups, angry prospects, or trust broken. However, push the number of requests to three times, or four, and now we have a much higher chance of losing trust with the people on the other end of the line. Every additional time they say "no" and we press on without empathy and/or push our agenda, trust is lost little by little, until we've gone past the point of no return. Prospects feel pressured, pushed, and jaded even more by yet another salesperson. Our line, then, is two "asks". It is a delicate line to walk and takes heightened awareness as a cold caller to identify this moment and take the best step without being pushy.

DEFEND THE FORT FIERCELY WITHOUT THROWING STONES

Sometimes in our profession, we are looked at as the scum of the earth. Prospects love to take out their rage and project it at us. I think as part of the H2H Sales Values, we need to help prospects shift their mindset to respect salespeople as true professionals who can help change people and companies for the better.

How do we do that? It begins by respecting ourselves and taking pride in what we do. It's then standing our ground. By calling out negative language or tones, we can build back respect with potential buyers. If we let prospects walk all over us because "the customer is always right," then they're going to continue acting that way toward every salesperson they interact with. Often, standing our ground can even win them back over. They don't expect that type of response; realizing their ego got in the way can open up their ears.

Fierce is unique because it could be considered a nuance of cold call execution. When prospects project negativity, resentment, and false accusations onto sales professionals, it adds an intensity to the caller's assertiveness. While this is rarely talked about in twenty-first-century sales, ferocity in our approach to negative biases can often go a long way towards healing prospects, even those who have suffered the most. Giving ourselves permission to defend our interest in building trust allows us to speak at the same level as high-level executive prospects who are passing their hurt to us. The challenge is in separating the person from the problem.

Choice of words is crucial here, as we need to not throw stones. Remember, we are attempting to build trust as quickly as possible, and sometimes this means attacking issues brought up by our prospects that are unfounded or need to be reframed to help them better understand the truth about a topic.

For example, let's just say I'm representing SHP. I call a prospect and get the person I'm looking for on the phone. I share my name, company, and a one-line introduction to what I do. As I begin to ask them my Hone-in question, they yell aggressively without any reason or explanation.

"I'm not interested in telemarketing companies!" they say. "Y'all suck!"

And yet, they stay on the line.

Now, if I wanted to be defensive and cause harm to my prospect, I could respond in kind, with a cool "Well someone is cranky today!" Clearly, this wouldn't go well. However, I understand why a salesperson, who is being attacked for simply doing their job, would feel defensive at this moment. After all, the prospect chose to answer the call when they could have declined it. But unfortunately, instinctive and defensive reactions aimed back at the prospect will harm the relationship. These reactions do the opposite of building trust.

While there are certainly better ways most of us have used to respond to this "nail-in-the-coffin" type of answer from our prospects, there is a way to clap back without losing trust that can actually give you a chance of continuing the conversation. While it appears there is nowhere to go when the prospect immediately says they aren't interested and attacks your business early in the conversation, the opposite could be true. You could just be dealing with your prospect's emotional reaction since you caught them off guard, and they might have interest. In fact, it sounds as though they may have used a company like SHP before to know "ya'll suck." Furthermore, they freely picked up the phone. While they may have been busy, you didn't interrupt or do anything wrong by calling. You simply reached out to them (assuming you followed proper federal and state compliance laws, of course). So, why should you stand for the abuse and just eat it, time after time? This is where this value has purpose and embodies self-respect for the sales person. It's tough to continuously be beaten down with no recourse, consistently submitting to aggression and anger for something you didn't do. You can only take so much. The tragedy is some leave the field because of this. The cure can be this H2H Sales Value. If we can fiercely defend the fort at the right moments without throwing stones, it can many times fill up our cup, providing us energy and the power to keep going.

When the prospect has a resentment-filled emotional response, sometimes the best way to diffuse, while still putting up defenses and showing self-respect, is to respond fiercely to any perceived false claims, while offering logic and solutions that could help them. For instance, what if my response to "I'm not interested!!!" was, (mind you, in a calm, cool, yet fast-paced tone), "I can understand, but I haven't even had the opportunity to share with you how we can help. I'm asking if you've considered this solution because we work with other companies like yours and have made an impact."

Pausing there to wait for their response puts the ball in their court and has them in a mental pickle. They likely didn't expect me to hold my ground in such a professional way—one that reflects I am not a subservient, lower-level telemarketer they can simply squash with satisfaction like a bug on the floor. In fact, by standing my ground, not only do I surprise them, but I also open up their mind, because I have responded with logic they didn't follow. If I say, "I don't understand how you can determine we suck without even knowing exactly how we work and how we can help," quickly, in stride, at a cool, curious tone and pause, it matches their offense with a layer of self-respect and stuns them with logic. If they double down on their negativity, it'll be obvious to everyone, especially themselves, that they are stuck in anger without any reason behind it. It'll make them think, and it has the ability to unwind their actions and actually give you an opportunity to continue the conversation.

CONFIDENT, NOT CONCEITED

Confidence is a hard trait to pinpoint as it is the careful balance of competence delivered with humility. Confidence can do wonders in transferring belief to prospects. They need to know how they can be helped while simultaneously being treated with respect for their position of "not knowing" the value of your offering. One problem in the sales profession has always been inflated egos. When confidence in producing results turns to arrogance, people tend to stop learning and begin moving backwards in their willingness to listen. In selling scenarios, this can be projected as an egocentric personality onto the prospects. This can be communicated as things being more about the salesperson than about the prospect.

Arrogance can range from subtle comments to pretentious statements to prospects. Here are a few examples of statements I've heard salespeople say that exude conceit, overshadowing any confidence that could have been transmitted instead:

1. "I'd love to set up a time to show you how what we have is much better than what you have currently."
2. "What is your budget? I don't want to waste my time here."

3. "How do I speak to someone in a higher position than you to sell them my product?"
4. "If you don't sign this, I won't hit my numbers. Do me a solid here."
5. "I have xx years of experience in this industry. I think I know what I'm talking about."

From the prospect's perspective, they are looking to feel helped, not hurt or vulnerable. Using these examples, we can change our language to be more confident with similar messages. Here is how the examples above could be changed to confident statements rather than conceited ones.

- Instead of 1, say, "Are you open to setting up a time to meet to show you how we may be different from who you are currently using, even if it is just to provide options for the future?"
- Instead of 2, say, "If you have a few minutes, I can set up a time to share with you our pricing to see if this is something that could work with your budget?"
- Instead of 3, say, "Are you in charge of x area? Happy to share with you if you are. If not, who is in charge of x there?"
- Instead of 4, say, "I was following up to see if we are still aligned on the "go" date so we can prepare our team the best for you. Are you still on pace for the [DATE]?"
- Instead of 5, say, "We do have some accomplishments and references that could help give you confidence in our work. I'd be happy to send a case study or reference. Which one would be better to share with you to give you the confidence you need?"

Confidence changes how the prospect receives the info so trust can be built more quickly. Arrogance poses more questions and shuts off the prospect from trust needed to make a sale. Being aware of how we interact with prospects can help us determine if we lean more on one side of this coin or the other. The changes can range from a slight language adjustment to a massive attitude shift.

EMOTIONAL INTELLIGENCE (EQ)

While its popularity has been on the rise, one of the most practical, but easily overlooked modern sales people skills is EQ in selling. Utilizing emotional intelligence is a super skill and a gift. Without it, we are less human, dynamic, and effective in business relationships. EQ enables us to identify and manage our own emotions to read and influence the emotions of others. Jeb Blout says ". . . *sales-specific* emotional intelligence on sales performance can no longer be ignored. Buyers are starving for authentic human interaction. In our tech-dominated society, interpersonal skills (responding to and managing the emotions of others) and interpersonal skills (managing your own disruptive emotions) are more essential to success in sales than at any point in history."[1] There is a wide variety of skills and practices to deploy by being aware of while using EQ. At the time the book *Sales EQ* hit the shelves, the topic was revolutionary in the industry. It was only an emerging topic in the sales profession at the time, but the book pointed to EQ as a critical skill needed in conversations to build rapport, relationships, and to achieve maximum results.

In addition, Daniel Goleman's book *Emotional Intelligence*[2] was one of the originals on the topic published in 1995 and has had a unique and real impact on The H2H Method™.

While "tonality" and "mirroring" have become nomenclature in sales vocab, Goleman uses the terms *attunement* and *emotional entrainment* as a way to define how there can be influence through emotional tone and moods. In fact, he says "the coordination of moods is the essence of rapport." Goleman says this about the impact of *emotional entrainment*: "Setting the emotional tone of an interaction is, in a sense, a sign of dominance at a deep and intimate level. It means driving the emotional state of another person. Emotional entrainment is the heart of influence."

I love this definition of *emotional entrainment* because it gives us a perspective of what tonality and mirroring our prospects' emotions can accomplish in sales. Matching emotion demonstrates an awareness of the other person's state. By speaking at their level emotionally, we can build trust much more quickly and move to vulnerability, openness, and ultimately, a relationship.

For example, if we're on the phone with a prospect who sounds a bit stoic and isn't showing much emotion, we need to match this state. If our prospect is more energetic, uses inflection in their voice, or sounds excited, then we need to turn up our levels to meet them there within the best of our ability.

Emotional entrainment is just one way EQ is applied in sales, but EQ has become so relevant it's a part of the H2H values required to have success with cold phone calls in twenty-first-century sales conversations.

CHAPTER 19
H2H SELLING VALUE STATEMENT

A value statement gives us a long-term, high-level perspective on the set of principles we live by as we practice our work. Many companies establish a value statement through a corporate lens, but here we are zooming in to provide a more granular code of action to guide our behavior and speech within the bounds of the sales profession.

For many sales organizations, value statements aren't typically established as an applicable and practical piece to the puzzle in successful selling relationships in today's selling landscape. If anything, they are loosely connected to a global corporate value statement unrelated to the activities on the sales floor. We are trying to reverse that trend and make it specific to a department.

Here's the value statement for The H2H Method™:

To consistently define and fulfill what it means to have human-to-human selling values while striving for highest performance in twenty-first-century selling and business relationships.

Let's break that down.

Our value statement provides a theme that guides what we do. It also gives us an ideal—ongoing effort—to continually strive toward. Specific words are crafted to draw out desirable traits in our work. For instance, *define* empowers us to observe and analyze the words we use in an effort to find the most truth in our vocabulary and actions when we sell, while *fulfill* has to do with committing to action and building trust when we are speaking with team members, prospects, and clients.

As we go out into the marketplace, we find it is always shifting and changing. It's necessary to keep our ears to the ground so we can appreciate what's going on and make corresponding shifts as needed. Like any business, we need to stay relevant. Remember our example about those utterly irrelevant black-and-white TVs? The company offering them lacked critical awareness about what was needed in the marketplace. In the same vein, we need products or services that are relevant. Otherwise, our prospects will have a hard time trusting anything we're talking about (even if they like us and how we went about contacting them). This is an effort to maximize performance mind you. If we are just shifting to building friendships but not partnerships, then we aren't making money and clients aren't receiving value. Performance and trust are our north stars and the value statement is the compass to get us there. Consistently defining, learning, and redefining H2H values enables us to stay sharp when engaging in those meaningful conversations with prospects and continually build trust.

CHAPTER 20
H2H SELLING CHARACTERISTICS

Characteristics refer to specific nuances of conversation that communicate our values and objectives to prospects in digestible, persuasive ways. Remember, our role as salespeople is to evangelize and reel in our prospects as we help them believe in our offering's value. (This *is* selling, after all.)

H2H Characteristics are designed to provide structure and borders around the way we disseminate information. They strengthen our efforts, creating optimal impact by providing conversational "bone" instead of "fat." Let's review a few of these vital fundamentals.

THE FEWER THE ADJECTIVES, THE BETTER

Too many adjectives are off-putting, but action verbs structure a conversation with logic and value. Think: fewer "fat" words such as "excellent" and "maximum", and more "bone" words such as "increases" or "saves." Trimming the fat this way communicates your value to the prospect clearly and tangibly. If you were to talk to your prospect by saying, "You're going to love our service! It's amazing! It's great! It is so fantastic! Do you want to buy it?" the answer will likely be a version of "Yeah—not so much." However, deploying action verbs may sound something like, "What's unique about our offering is it connects you to buyers more quickly than traditional methods, increasing your revenue by 25 percent or more." You may not have closed a deal here, but you are certainly enabling them to conceptualize and feel the potential impact of your offering.

Sometimes, it can be difficult to avoid using adjectives completely. When this is the case, just be sure to back up an adjective with a fact, feature, or metric everyone can agree on. For instance, if you have "the best customer service," then give a reason how that would make sense for your prospect. Do you have the best customer service because you said so? Or, do you have the best customer service because you will reply to any question or comment within 1 hour, a standard no one else can keep in the industry? Using adjectives can work, but the more you use them, the more you need to back up your word; otherwise, it can sound like fluff with no substance. *Remember, we don't mind if the prospect knows we are selling them something. We just don't want them to feel like it.*

In summary, adjectives can make the prospect feel the sales person, product, and process is salesy, pushy, and selfish. Verbs deliver action and belief that your offering can help them.

CONVERSATION, NOT "CONTENT."

Conversations are not content written for reading consumption. When I consult our clients on scripts, I walk them backwards through their pitch to reframe their idea of sales conversations. This is because cold phone conversations are less like a dissertation and more like the way you speak to someone at a bar, party, or when you're first meeting them at a networking event. My favorite approach is to explain what you do the same way you would describe it to your grandmother. In other words, break down your high-level vocabulary so the prospect can easily digest what you're saying the first time you speak with them.

Translating sales value into layperson's speak in a live conversation format is much easier said than done. When we write, we often do not naturally write the way we talk. We use bigger words, we contemplate the exact award-winning line, and we add complexity. All those things have their place, but that place *isn't* in natural conversation, where it creates a disingenuous and sometimes outright unrealistic impression on the person you're talking to. I cannot stress this next part enough: use caution with your language. Even when elevated language is authentic, it can start to sound like a sales call. When that happens, it actually triggers the salesperson stigma. (And, as we all know by now, *literally no one wants that.*)

However, I will offer one caveat about using simplified language: depending on the industry we're calling into, it can place limitations on the way we communicate—and that means it isn't always the best way forward. For example, if we're talking with individuals in high-level positions at certain companies, we might actually *need* to explain our offering using more industry jargon. In those instances, we're not just matching the tone and emotion of the prospect. We are also matching the language they speak.

That said, even if the situation calls for raising our vocabulary, it doesn't mean we need to, or even should, go into great detail. We simply need to say enough that a prospect can understand our value from a high-level perspective before we talk with them further down the road. For instance, at SHP, we might want to stay away from, "Hi, my name is Ryan, and we offer sales development conversations to accelerate the top of your pipeline funnel using our SDRs and XDRs." Instead, we use words and phrases they're more likely to be familiar with: "Hi, my name is Ryan with SHP, and we provide cold call appointment-setting specifically for companies like yours to help you increase your leads so you can continue to grow."

Attempting to sound like a thought leader when you speak can actually create more obstacles in the conversation because it simply *takes too long*. Consider: using layperson's terms is not just about the risk of sounding like content. Clear, simple, direct speech simply helps a prospect digest your information as quickly as possible. Were they expecting your call? No. Were they busy when you called them? Yes. Quickly getting to the point can encourage them to feel like you're respecting their time—because you are.

CONVERSATION CADENCE

What is a sales conversation? Well, for one thing, it's not a harangue. It's not an investor pitch session. It's not your soapbox to announce your abilities in whatever it is you do and excel in. Sales conversations are dialogues with another human being. Effective or healthy conversation with your friend, counselor, or coworker typically adopts a natural rhythm or cadence that follows a pattern: *comment, question, response, question, response, etc.* As time and conversation advance, so does rapport, allowing a relationship to build. This is the anatomy of a cold conversation.

This format creates opportunities for more time on the phone, and more time on the phone equals more opportunity to build the trust needed for a healthy conversational exchange. When I speak, I need to pause and offer you a chance to respond. When I ask a question, I need to listen and wait for you to finish. This natural reciprocation sets the pace of the conversation.

TONE TEKKERS

We've talked about how tonality and mirroring is the heart of influence. If we can get on the emotional level of the prospect, they can feel like they're heard and might give us more opportunity to speak to them about something we think can help them. Mirroring and adapting tone to positively match our prospect's are key cold calling characteristics in these highly dynamic conversations that take conversions from 0 to 1 in a business relationship. Tone Tekkers is all about utilizing our tone as a skill for building trust and rapport with prospects on the phone.

Have you heard of the 7-38-55% Rule developed by Albert

Mehrabian? This rule is a breakdown of the percentages representing disparate forms of communication "likened" from a person you're face-to-face with. The idea is a person you're speaking to face-to-face determines their "likening" of you broken down in 3 ways—adding up to 100. The first 7% is transmitted through words, 38% through tone, and 55% through body language.[1] In theory, if we transition this rule to a phone conversation, the body language percentage is out altogether (clearly, we can't see the person on the other end of a phone call). By process of elimination then, only words, and tone remain in a prospect determining if they like us or not! How you say things matters! Daniel Goleman says this about the impact of nonverbal communication:

> Just as the mode of the rational mind is words, the mode of the emotions is nonverbal. Indeed, when a person's words disagree with what is conveyed via his tone of voice, gesture, or other nonverbal channel, the emotional truth is in how he says something rather than what he says. One rule of thumb used in communications research is that 90 percent or more of an emotional message is nonverbal.[2]

The application of first listening to the tone of our prospects and then matching the tone when we speak can have a significant positive effect on the results of our cold calls. It's admittedly not an easy task. I've come across countless decision makers who surprise me with the energy they bring to a call. I remember one time I called a prospect who was a CFO. He answered in a sad, slow, and drawn-out voice with little life: "This . . . is . . . Rob (pause)." Wow! That took me by surprise. Either this guy was having a really bad day, eternally hated his job, or just innately spoke at the same pace as a sloth moves up a tree. How do you respond to someone like that? Do you try to win them out of a bad mood? Do you try to liven them up? No! Quite the opposite.

Remember, our goal is to build trust, spark interest in what we do, and generate top-performing results. Successful cold calls are either functions of good instinct or trained intuition, so it's crucial to not react to an energy you weren't expecting. At that moment, it's critical to accept the person as they are and adapt and use entrainment to match their energy. In this situation, I had to take a breath and really calm my energy down. By slowing my mind and getting on the same page, I stood a better chance of advancing the conversation, and as a result, starting a relationship with this person and winning the opportunity to influence them. I should note as well that these calls don't always result in an appointment and ensuing sale. However, they do, more times than not, *lengthen the conversation.* This means conversations stuck in the beginning would go to the middle, those in the middle move to some minimal next step. And minimal next steps turn to ideal next steps.

ELIMINATES ALL DECEPTION

By now we know that cold contact with prospects invariably bumps up against the natural resistance built by years of *poor sales ethics.* So when you call your prospect, regardless of how amazing a salesperson you are, how truthful or honest, or how much you can help them, building trust and diffusing the salesperson stigma will always mean a barrier to work through. We have to use transparency, honesty, and EQ to help diffuse the stigma and build trust back if we want to begin a sales journey with them.

That said, we also have to abstain from pretending, deceiving, getting over on, or slighting our prospects.

There are a few ways to eliminate deception. One is to be upfront about what type of call they've just answered. In fact, clarifying the type of call early on can disarm them. By taking away the power they have to call you out on a "sleazy sales call," they have to fish for other reasons to get off the phone (or it can simply stop them in their tracks since you beat them to the punchline). Clarity does more than disarm a prospect, though—it signals that you're there to earn their trust. Plus, you did something they didn't expect in such a positive way that it buys you time.

This can work in gatekeeper and decision maker conversations, as well. For example, if I'm calling to ask for Laura, get the gate-keeper on the phone, and promptly eliminate all deception, a conversation might go something like this:

"Hi, is Laura there?"

"Yeah, she's here. But what's this call regarding?"

"Yeah, absolutely. This is Ryan, and I'm with Superhuman Prospecting. I'll be transparent. This is a sales partnership call. We help businesses like yours with cold call appointment setting. I want to see if we might be a good fit for your organization some-time down the road."

Conducting a call that way can dispel suspicions fueled by a need to fish out the "real" reason behind my call. It also increases my chance of having success with the company. My transparency puts the ball in their court; suddenly, they have to make a decision: *Is this caller dangerous for the decision maker? Or, based on what the caller said, is this something that we can use?*

Diffusing the *salesperson stigma* can also help us identify whether the gatekeeper might actually be a stakeholder. Your efforts to build trust may encourage them to pass you to the right person. But regardless of which part of the sales process you are in or whom you're talking to at the prospect's company, you might have just opened up their ear to ways you can help their business.

SECTION FOUR
GET PRACTICAL, GET TACTICAL

CHAPTER 21
H2H TACTICAL APPROACH

All right! You've made it through the philosophical, strategic, and principles portion of the book! Nice work! If you have read all the way through the first three sections, my hope is that you now (at least partially) view cold calling through a new lens. Your perspective should be at least widened, if not changed. If you have skipped the beginning and moved directly to this part, you will still reap many of the benefits of the methodology; however, you may be at a slight disadvantage. You may view the following as a "standard" or "templated" approach, only accepting tactics and techniques as "another" option in your arsenal of scripts and methods toolbox. But the full impact of H2H comes from an adoption of multiple layers of cold calling, not just scripting and conversation language.

The benefits of this method also increase the more it is in use. It's a foundation to conversation building toward higher levels of performance as experience and repetitions increase. Why can you become better and better the more you use this method? Adopting these principles widens possibilities by providing freedom of personality, candor, and authenticity while maintaining guidelines in business relationship building. This section is all about the practical strategies, tactics, and technique applied to call conversation and script frameworks.

After thousands of campaigns run in dozens of industries, we've tested, evolved, identified, and now have labeled some flexible yet vital parts of a successful and quality cold call relevant to twenty-first-century sales development conversations. These components act as elements to most any true cold phone conversation, adding value to the prospect and their business. We call these the Four Core Components of a Cold Call (4CX4).

The 4CX4 is a framework built for understanding how a human conversation works in a structured, conversational format. Using our human-to-human mission, think of these elements of a conversation as the bones. With all the tricks, jokes, and one-liners stripped away, this is what we have left. The four components are the Quick Prop (QP), the Hone-in (Hi), the Calling Prop (CP), and the Next Steps (NXTS).

In studying thousands of cold call conversations from dozens of industries, we have found the most successful scripts boil down to three distinctive script structures for decision maker or stakeholder conversations. The three frameworks are The Consultative Conversation Framework (CCF), The No-Bull Script, and The Survey Script.

When searching for content or how to cold call, what one typically finds are some general theories or ideas on how to conduct these conversations, including some steps appearing similar to The H2H Method™. We've also found a significant amount of content around parts of a call. For example, we see a lot of commentary on introductions and opening lines, as well as objections and rebuttals. Most of the time, though, we find little in the way of a complete philosophy behind a style (other than some rules of thumb or actions to avoid). By contrast, in The H2H Method™, every component, as mentioned in our Trust Umbrella, leads back to building trust and a strategy for moving prospects forward while maintaining relationships.

Likewise, in the following sections, pay specific attention to how each part of these components has a specific purpose. When you reach a specific milestone within the conversation, you'll remember the context and the direction to not only help your potential customer, but also help yourself. At SHP, we've been collecting data since 2018 to map successful frameworks in the marketplace, regardless of the industry. We've called from over 50 primary business industries over that time and have been able to empirically track responses.

One note before we begin some of the technical portions of this book: any cold call framework we recommend is located in a call where we have moved past the gatekeeper conversation and are actively speaking to the decision maker conversation. The cold call conversation can be broken up into three parts: the gatekeeper conversation, the decision maker/stakeholder conversation, and the objections and responses section. The three cold call frameworks we will discuss apply to the part of a cold call when a decision maker/stakeholder connection has been made and a conversation is initiated by the caller.

CHAPTER 22
CONSULTATIVE CONVERSATION FRAMEWORK (CCF)

T he 4CX4 structure gives sales development reps (SDRs) a leg up because it acts both as a guardrail and conversation steps as SDRs move toward the end goal of the call. This structure enables SDRs to focus and build muscle memory around the steps they should guide their prospect through while building trust and value.

The 4CX4 component combination for the CCF is a conversation structure that has been developed by studying tens of thousands of conversations and thousands of appointments or "next steps" identified. It's the framework found most commonly in our B2B sales development conversations, and it is designed to follow specific human-to-human conversation exchange types. The person initiating comments asks a question, the recipient answers, the first person responds, and there are questions from both sides. This continues until a point is given, taken, or learned. The components and subcomponents within the 4CX4 boil down the conversation's flow into different pieces that can be labeled for context and summarized in any given sales-development cold phone call.

The 4CX4 order for this conversation formation is as follows:

1. QP - Quick Prop
2. Hi - Hone-in (Bridge Statements)
3. CP - Calling Prop (Discovery Questions and Extended Prop)
4. NXTS - Next Steps (Qualifying Questions)

Before we dive into each component and subcomponent, follow this big-picture explanation of how the design works. It'll help maintain perspective as we touch on each component and part of the conversation.

- The CCF is designed to give conversation leadership to the SDR, while providing opportunities for the prospect to follow and engage freely.
- When the SDR first reaches the prospect on the phone, the conversation begins with the Quick Prop (QP). The QP is a quick description of what the offering is with a light feature or benefit.
- The Hone-in (Hi) is a very specific discovery question to engage the prospect and is the first sign of an open conversation. The Bridge Statements provide programmed ledges and opportunity for the SDR to respond regardless of the Hi answer.
- The Calling Prop (CP) is the pinnacle of the conversation providing the most value to our prospect.
- The Discovery Questions subcomponent re-engages the prospect after we have spoken.
- The Extended Prop subcomponent gives the SDR more value, explanation, or points about the offering if the prospect wants to hear more or is in need of specific value missed in the CP.
- Lastly, the Next Steps (NXTS), identifies what the next best step is along the sales cycle as it matches the buying journey of the prospect.

The four primary components can be shifted and moved

around, but they provide us with some foundational steps in building trust between 0 and 1 in business relationships. Also, our scripts are written linearly. Since we are all primarily on computers when we cold call, we have found linear to be a more natural way for eyes to flow and mice to scroll. Writing linear scripts versus tree diagrams provides salespeople with a more ergonomic functionality. While we use tree diagrams for a big picture strategy view, we use linear scripts for a more functional and efficient approach.

QP - QUICK PROP

Each component contains an anatomy called an API. In this acronym, A stands for Assumption, P for Purpose, and I for Instruction. This granular approach empowers us to understand where we are along our journey in a conversation with a prospect.

The image below provides a summary of the QP's API. Review this image for a roll-up of each point before moving to the Hone-in.

QP | Quick Prop

- (A)ssumptions
  - Stigma against salespeople
  - Not expecting call / busy
- (P)urpose
  - Right frame of mind
  - Get past first few seconds
- (I)nstruction
  - State what you do & light feature/benefit

Once we truly grasp each component and subcomponent, we can act more freely in our conversations. We pause and think less. We act more on intuition. Both of these shifts enable us to bring our own individual personality and style into these conversations. One of the misconceptions about scripts is that they must be said word for word, in a specific tone, in order to be properly executed. Our research and extensive practice shows how ineffective that rote approach actually is. Following components while maintaining a fluid conversation takes some practice, but once you've learned to touch these primary components conversationally, adapting your own personality to them becomes natural. This is where we find the most success.

So, let's talk about the QP and its API, specifically. The QP, or Quick Prop, is a description of what is provided by the company's offering, with the addition of a shortly explained benefit or feature. The *assumption*, or A of the QP's API, has two parts. The first is that the prospect is already biased against salespeople because of the *salesperson stigma*. We have to keep this in the back of our minds: when we get on the phone, we're going to start in a negative mental position with the prospect. That understanding guides the way we move forward. See, when they roll the dice to answer your call, it could be one of many calls they have to answer! It could be a customer, a friend, a partner, a family member, or a sales call! The list goes on. When a prospect answers the phone and realizes they're on a sales call, the stigma can kick in quickly—making it more difficult for SDRs to move forward. This situation can be daunting, but it doesn't mean the prospect won't talk to you. Many times, it just signifies that they're not going to give you all the time in the world to state the purpose of your call and how you can help them.

Training ourselves to think this way can give us a leg up, because we know every call requires us to work our way out of a hole.

The second assumption, then, is to presume the individual we hope to have a conversation with not only doesn't know us, but they also don't expect our call. Conjecturing that the prospect is also a busy person underscores the fact that we're not going to have much time to get our point across and help build value. However, understanding they're busy allows us to move through the conversation quickly, so we are in turn respecting their time. Translation: the fact they aren't expecting our call won't derail the entire train, but we need to proceed knowing those three obstacles —they are not expecting our call, they are also receiving a call from someone who would eventually like to sell them something, and they're extremely busy decision makers—are already bolted to the tracks ahead.

Phew! This first cold phone call can be a lot to handle, for both sides!

Admittedly, each new call puts salespeople in a tough position. But, that's why you're reading, right? The QP technique, when followed, can help transition an uncomfortable situation into an easy, potential-filled conversation.

> NOTE: There's a myth out there about cold calling your prospects that states when cold callers or sales developers reach out to decision makers and they answer, these sales people are interrupting their day. Whoa. This is quite an accusation!
>
> Here at H2H we believe this couldn't be further from the truth, and we can explain. First, let's back up. When we called them, did we force them to pick up the phone? No, they freely and willingly decided to stop what they were doing, look at the inbound phone number pop-up on their phone, and voluntarily answer it. As we've stated, these folks are smart enough to know the possibilities of what can happen when there is an unknown, unlabeled, and unsaved number calling them. So if they chose to pick up the phone, they have given us permission to talk to them, full stop. Don't let the noise convince you otherwise. If you believe you have interrupted someone's day, then you've bought into the lie that the people you are calling are more important than you and what you can offer them. This is simply untrue, especially if you believe in what and who you are evan-gelizing.
>
> Salespeople must believe in what they are selling to be successful and top performers. If we believe what we are offering can truly help our prospects, then businesspeople, who buy and sell every day to survive and thrive in business, need products and services that can

help them. Maybe, just maybe, you have the perfect offering for them. By taking the opportunity at hand when the prospect picks up the phone, you are instantly in a position to help.

I can't overstate this fact: believing your product is worth a busy prospect's time is your choice. You can choose not to believe it. At that point, however, you may actually be interrupting their day with a cold call full of worthless spam. Perhaps a true interruption of someone's day is calling them when you believe you are and don't think you can help them.

The *P, or purpose* in the API, is much simpler than you might think. We don't need to have a full monologue prepared! Remember, if we assume the prospect is not expecting our call, then are they fully aware and present to digest what it is we do, how it works, the features, benefits, and all our accolades? Impossible!

Our purpose is first to play defense as we help them transition their thoughts into the right frame of mind to hear what we're saying, and second (and this might surprise you), to just get through the first few seconds! A lot of salespeople get this wrong because they try to word vomit and overpower the prospect in the first seven seconds of the call. This is not it.

Acknowledging we are in a defensive position in the QP reframes our mindset. So our aim then is to shift them to what we're talking about and get past the first few seconds. By playing defense in the beginning, it eases the friction and allows us to then open up the conversation later, giving us the best chance of success in the direction we're hoping the conversation will go.

Lastly is *I, instruction.* With the *assumption* and *purpose* in perspective, can you already begin to imagine what the *instruction* of the words might be? All that is needed is to simply state what you do with a light benefit or feature. And that's it. By doing this, we are adjusting the attention of the prospect to what we do. Here's an example of what a QP with the API in place might look like at SHP:

Quick Prop** [Component 1]:

Hi my name is _____ with Superhuman Prospecting. We provide outsourced cold calling and appointment setting to companies across the United States to help them generate more leads for their sales pipeline.

That's it! That is all you have to say. It's a simple description with a light benefit, shifting their mind to understand what you are talking about. Notice we didn't start off with any extravagant tricks or one-liners. Remember, we don't mind if they know this is a sales call. We just don't want them to feel like it's a salesy one meant to lure them towards something they don't want to be involved in later. In addition, by delivering a simple phrase they can digest quickly, you can often hold their attention before their brain starts to wander or become skeptical about what your schtick is going to be and what "amazing" offer you'll turn onto them.

Note, too, that this QP doesn't have any greeting or permission in its foundation; we simply dive right in. Many professionals choose to input *preferential add-ons* fitting their personality here. These are crutches and relationship-builders that can certainly warm up the conversation, but many are geared toward making the SDR feel comfortable, when they should be focused on the prospect. If you feel uncomfortable going right into your QP at first, this is completely normal. Leading a conversation can disrupt the perception you want to have: that this call will feel like a normal conversation with your friends or family. In that case, natural icebreakers can help diffuse the tension. However, my recommendation is to only use these as needed, rather than as a cemented step in every QP you engage in. The following are a few *preferential add-ons* you can attach to the beginning of the QP as you see fit:

- "Hi [Decision Maker Name], how are you?"
- "Hi [Decision Maker Name], how have you been?"
- "I understand you're busy right now, but . . ."
- "Is this a good time to talk?"
- "I didn't catch you at a bad time, did I?"

- "Do you have a moment to speak?"
- "I'll be up front with you, this is a cold call."
- "Do you have 26 seconds to hear why I called?"

While not required for success, these add-ons can ease the pressure. Keep in mind, though, that they do add time to the QP. Since one of our purposes is to get past the first few seconds and reach the Hone-in, add-ons can sometimes work against our goals by adding time to the call that we don't have, lowering our chances the prospect will stay on call much longer.

HI - HONE-IN

The Hone-in (Hi) is an ensuing discovery question almost immediately following the QP, typically said in one fell swoop along with it. We'll need to be prepared with our answer regardless of what the prospect says. Fortunately, this specific question design makes up a large portion of scripts we write at H2H and SHP. If the Hi question is asked in the way we suggest, any answer to the question will be sufficient to bridge us to the Calling Prop.

Hi | Hone-in

- (A)ssumptions
  - Prospect business can improve or is experiencing pain
  - Asking questions lengthens conversations
- (P)urpose
  - Leads them into a conversation
  - Identify use status of product/service
- (I)nstruction
  - Ask question directed at around pain
  - Ask about familiarity with product or service

As we approach this part of the conversation, there are two basic *assumptions* as a part of our API. The first is that we are going to assume the prospect's business can improve or is experiencing some type of pain that we can potentially fix. Second, we assume that asking questions lengthens conversations.

This question has a few *purposes*. Recall from our discussions about QP that we provide a quick description with a briefly stated benefit or feature; this should be followed immediately by a Hi question, because the less time we spend talking, the more time we have to diffuse the *salesperson stigma* by giving our prospect an opportunity to speak.

The first purpose, then, is to start a conversation—to get your prospect talking! As shown in the Conversion Probability Timeline graphic, the longer we are in a conversation, the better chance we have of converting a prospect to next steps. Conversations build trust, and longer conversations set up quality next steps more effectively and reliably than short conversations.

The second purpose of Hi is to learn about the use status of the product or service we are calling about. By asking the prospect if they have used a product or service like ours, or if they have considered it, we narrow their possible answers down to a select few. Our question might uncover a pain point our offering can solve—a bad relationship with a similar product or service as ours or other related responses that help us identify how and what to speak to next. These two purposes of our Hi reduce friction and make it easier for the prospect to continue the conversation while providing us with valuable information, as well.

The *instruction* here includes two parts. First, ask a question directed around the prospect's pain, if possible. Second, ask about the familiarity of the product or service we're calling about.

If I were calling for SHP, I would state my QP and then move immediately into the Hi. Here is how that would look:

Hone-in** [Component 2]:

Are you using an outsourced lead generation solution currently to help continue your growth or have you considered it in the past?

While speaking, it may sound as if the QP and the Hi are one.

Depending on the situation, a pause may make sense, but movement together gets the point across quickly and starts a conversation.

While not explicit in this Hi, mentioning a light benefit can also uncover a pain. Notice how we say "help continue your growth." While some Hi questions may add a bit more of a painful dose to the question, stating something as we want it, or as an ideal, can naturally draw out opposite feelings if the ideal is not met. Another way to say this with more emphasis on pain could be "Are you using an outsourced, lead generation solution currently to avoid losing control of your leads flow so you can grow as you'd like, or have you considered a solution like this in the past?"

Sometimes I imagine the Hi question similar to the vibe you look for with someone when you first meet them. Whether it's on a date, someone new joining your group of friends, or at a networking event, asking questions simply makes it easier to understand them so you know how to relate. You've heard these:

- "So, what do you like to do?"
- "Do you like to play sports? Or, do you like art? Do you like film?"

The problem I see in modern cold phone conversations is that sales people like to disqualify themselves at this part of the conversation by asking questions that limit the positive answers that could naturally arise from the question. Imagine if I called and said, "Hi, this is Ryan with Superhuman Prospecting. We do cold call appointment-setting for companies like yours. Would you be interested in using our service?"

Yikes.

That approach takes a huge risk. Logically, based on our API, it does not make sense to continue if the prospect says "no" (unless of course you are calling to talk about something else completely at that point). You're just going to go ahead and ask if they're interested in using your service in the first 30 seconds of meeting them? I mean, you're assuming they're ready for this type of situation and that they've been waiting by the phone for someone to call. You don't know the type of experiences they've had. You don't know if they've had a bad time with another company. They don't know the value you can provide or how your offering works. It's already extremely difficult to get past the first few seconds when meeting someone cold. If this is the case, why limit the direction of the conversation?

So, if we agree it's best to ask a question that encourages more positive responses and fewer negative ones, then it's safe to assume the question we need to ask is an open-ended one, right?

Not quite.

In the first few seconds of meeting a prospect on a cold phone call, control is critical. We are leading the conversation. We called them, and we have a purpose when we call. Remember our objectives of a cold call? To spark interest in what we offer, to sell the next step, and to diffuse the *salesperson stigma.* Just like close-ended questions can stymie our conversation and halt progress, so can open-ended discovery questions this early in the conversation! Consider the open-ended question as, "what is your marketing strategy?" Imagine if I used this as my Hone-in question. "Hello, this is Ryan with Superhuman Prospecting. We do cold call appointment-setting for companies like yours. What is your marketing strategy?"

I'm sweating just thinking about asking this question. All the possible answers are starting to swarm, and no logic tree would be big enough to fit this in a Lucidchart tree diagram. Talk about anxiety attack! Not that you can't recover or work with the answers, but by virtue of asking the question, the chances an answer could throw you a curveball are higher. Think about our call again. My call is specific. It's a sales call. I have an objective. My conversation is strategic in nature. There is little time. I have to build trust with this prospect. By asking an open-ended question like this one, the possibilities can go anywhere, making it harder to harness the conversation, especially when we are just getting started in the conversation and our offering's value hasn't quite been delivered yet. Here are some possible answers to "what is your marketing strategy?" we'd have to be prepped to transition into our Calling Prop with regardless of how they respond:

- "We have a great one."
- "We don't have a great one."
- "We have one."
- "We rely on referrals."
- "We do a variety of things."
- "We have our own marketing team."
- "We run email campaigns."
- "We have used outsourced agencies."
- "We utilize Google Adwords."
- "We are successful with word-of-mouth."
- "Why do you care?"

And the list goes on. Even if you did receive this information, what would you do with it anyway in the first few seconds of a call? Would you ask how it's working for them? Would you transition to what you do since the conversation isn't moving toward cold call appointment setting? At this point, your logic tree has a higher chance of moving toward a potential "no" and a close-ended answer we didn't want anyway. Even If they are playing along, they can get the sense you aren't in control, or they don't know where it's going, rendering them uneasy or impatient.

This is why the Hi question is so effective when executed well. The logic behind it doesn't close prospects to a negative response, and it doesn't open up the can of worms to unlimited answers, tail-spinning the conversation out of control.

Let's go back to our original Hi question: "Have you used outsource cold calling and appointment-setting before, or have you considered it?" If I cut out the first open-ended question, I can jump right into this question, which we label a *balanced question*. *Balanced questions* find middle ground between a close-ended question that is either black or white and an open-ended question that gets you way off track.

The best way to create balance is to ask a question that (regardless of the prospect's response), will open a path to a value your offering can provide. Recall that in the Hi API, one purpose of the question is to identify the use status of the product or service we are calling about. We do this by asking a question that helps identify whether the prospect has used a product or service like yours. If they say they do use what we offer, you can easily move into the CP by saying something such as "That's great you use this product/service! We work better with those who already see the value in this." If they have not, you can answer with "Great, that's exactly why I'm reaching out" and then move into the same CP.

On the other hand, traditional questions such as "are you happy with this product or service" or "would you be interested in learning more," make it hard for you as a salesperson to find a path toward a longer conversation, especially when it is so early in the conversation and the prospect doesn't yet know the entire capacity of what you're offering. Asking a *balanced question* enables you to extend the conversation in a direction that could be mutually beneficial regardless of how the prospect responds. Let's unpack by learning the Bridge Statement.

Bridge Statement

The *bridge statement* is a segway response after any planned answer following the Hi. The Hi question is important to get right because, as we know by now, the conversation is still on rocks. In fact, we are still trying to earn the right to even have a conversation; the question we ask can move the conversation toward more, or sometimes and unfortunately, less. But if the prospect follows the logic of our question, their answer is always right!

Remember, most Hi questions ask if the prospect has used or considered using the product or service we represent. Whether they say yes or no, I'm okay with it! Both answers communicate the position I need to adopt so I can appropriately angle the rest of my conversation to meet their needs. If they are using a product or service like ours, revealing their familiarity with the product or service value, I know it can be easier to sell them later because the typical friction around product adoption has already been limited. On the other hand, if they haven't used the product, it can be just as positive of a response. The reason is because we know they aren't, or can't, be loyal to our competitor. First-to-use customers also often have love blinders on. They hear the value from you, and either don't look to other vendors or see the value enough with your offering to just say yes! The negative side to first-to-use customers is that there may be more of a struggle to adopt the offering because they don't know what the experience will be like. Remember though, regardless of their answer, I can work with whatever they throw at me, because they are participating in my conversation. Trust and interest are building.

Here are the basic responses to my Hone-in question, which can be customized and tailored to the product or service you're calling about and the market you're reaching out to:

Bridge Statement

[IF YES]:

Okay, that's good! I'm glad you understand how this is helpful for you. We typically work better with those who have something in place because they see the value.

We are a bit different though and can often compliment what you are already doing...

[IF NO]:

No problem, then this may be something to consider ...

The "IF YES" statement is when we acknowledge their use of a similar product. The power here is in the diffusing. It may seem logical that if the prospect answers with a "yes," that they use the product I'm offering, then maybe they could instinctively think they are "off the hook" from a sales call. However, that is not the direction the "IF YES" response ever goes. Remember, it can be a positive that they use a similar product because they are familiar with its value, and there can be less product education or adoption needed.

The "IF NO" statement is an easier logic for the salesperson to move with because it demonstrates a gap that the product or service could fill. But while it can feel better for the salesperson at this point, it can also be more difficult later for the sale. If we are cognizant of this fact, building more value, asking more questions, and proper follow-up may be needed for these opportunities. For now, store this new information in your short-term memory and begin to collect and organize which value you can share in the upcoming Calling Prop.

While it may seem as though the conversation is under complete control, we all know conversations can be unpredictable! Remember scripts are a guardrail or path, not a fixed train track. Sometimes, the HI can result in an objection, a request for more info, and a varied number of other responses we'll discuss how to work with later. The *bridge statement* provides your conversation with a logic tree to follow. It's the default, but not a required path of the conversation. As you practice this statement, the structure provides a box for you to think out of. The more you have a guide in your stride, the easier it becomes to reply off-the-cuff. Knowing how the conversation should go gives clarity when it goes off track.

CP - CALLING PROP

In the book *Influence*, author Robert Cialdini identifies a human psychological response called the "rule of reciprocity." The rule is that "we should try to repay what another person has provided us."[1] Applied to cold calling and sales, when we give someone a clear opportunity to have the floor and speak in selling conversation, the rule would suggest humans instinctively reciprocate and give the same opportunity back to the other. If we ask a question, we are giving that person an opportunity to let us have our turn when they are done answering. Cialdini states the rule is very powerful as well. He says, "One of the reasons reciprocation can be used so effectively as a device for gaining another's compliance is its power. The rule possesses awesome strength, often producing a yes response to a request that, except for an existing feeling of indebtedness, would have surely been refused."

> NOTE: *Clearly, I'm not suggesting unethical and deceptive use of the words here, but this psychological phenomenon alone provides enough for me to think about what and how much I am asking if I truly want to buy myself time and opportunity on a cold call.*

By design, then, we are starting conversations which create an environment for the rule of reciprocity to naturally work: by asking a *balanced question* of our prospect in the Hone-in, we give them an opportunity to speak; in turn, they give us an opportunity after. This is where the CP falls within this phenomenon perfectly.

CP | Calling Prop

- **(A)ssumptions**
  - ○ 1) Since they haven't ended call, there is opportunity to provide them value
  - ○ 2) Your time to shine!
- **(P)urpose**
  - ○ 1) Spark interest with prospect
- **(I)nstruction**
  - ○ 1) Deliver the "how" and "what"
  - ○ 2) Weave in Valuable Proposition Trifecta focused around answer from Hi

After the prospect has answered the Hi, they naturally pause and give you time to speak. The CP then is where we deliver the most value in relation to specifically how and why our product or service can help our prospect. By the time we get through the *bridge statement* and to the CP, we should have had time to build enough trust with them to hear how we can help. We have to depend on the fact they haven't hung up or asked to end the call as a sign we have built some level of rapport and trust. If we have made it through the first two steps, the ball does start to roll into your side of the court (This is discussed in the Conversion Probability Timeline a bit later). We are now out of a sales stigmatized hole and are beginning to take control of the conversation. This is your time to shine.

When considering our CP, we need to acknowledge what we say will depend on how the individual responds to the Hone-in. This is where we must have specific statements prepared that could be valuable to the prospect and their business. Communicating how our product or service works, the features, the ensuing benefits, as well as providing accolades, gives the prospect new understanding and perspective on why, what, and how you can help them. Listening intently during the Hi step can give us a direction to answer based on the different arrows we have in our quiver.

Here is an example of what one CP at SHP could look like:

...so the way it works is we help companies generate leads and appointments for their sales pipeline by making outbound calls and emails to their prospects through campaigns on a month-to-month basis.

- *Differentiating Feature: We have US-based sales development reps that work for you using the only comprehensive cold call method available from philosophy to frameworks.*
- *Tangible Benefit: We typically generate between 1 to 100 leads per month for our clients depending on the project size and industry*
- *Outstanding Accolade: We have done work for hundreds of SMBs up to companies such as AmerisourceBergen, Moen, Uber, and Amazon*

> *NOTE: In the script outlines we deploy in campaigns at SHP, we do include additional value bullets as seen above to use based on the direction of the conversation.*

We recommend stating the first line in the CP script at a minimum before customizing the conversation based on any information received in the Hone-in. If possible, describing how the offering or experience works provides a foundation for not only following logic to value, it also gives flexibility in "choosing your own adventure" just after. The reason for this is it will provide stability as you transition to delivering customized value. It also acts as a ledge statement, giving you a few seconds to collect your thoughts on what may be the best to answer with based on their

Hi response. To further drive home this point, you'll find the remainder of the "script" design and sub-components are typically listed in the script copy we design as "optional," even if recommended. This is because the more we speak with someone, the more the other end has time to think about their own situation and bring up topics outside of what is listed next in our linear component steps.

At this point, we hear quite a few things from our prospects, including listening noises, requests for more explanation, objections, questions, concerns, interest, and more. While the H2H Sales Scripts® for Cold Phone Calls scripts are written in a linear format, preparing to jump to the right location helps us react quickly and in stride in these moments. Remember, scripts are a guardrail. If the exchange gets "off-track," the script will allow you to get back on your path and move forward.

The CP API is chock full of substance for learning the Calling Prop component expertly. While many factors can define a successful call or call failure, the CP and its ensuing exchange can catalyze a moment of truth for the seller in moving prospects to next steps. What we read in the moment as relevant to, say, the value we chose to deliver, and how it is said all come to a head here. The API helps us as salespeople know how to prepare for this moment!

The *assumption* of the Calling Prop has two parts. First, as stated, if the prospect hasn't derailed or ended the call yet, there is an opportunity here to provide value. While some value or interest may have been sparked in the Quick Prop, we can't depend on it for full interest or curiosity in this Consultative Conversation Framework. At this point, we stop playing defense and go on the offensive.

The second *assumption* of the API is that the Calling Prop is your time to shine. While the entire call could be considered a performance, what happens after the Hi is going to be with the light shining on you. While the first *assumption* identifies the client is truly open to hearing value because they haven't ended the call, then this next *assumption* is the realization that you as the seller need to be prepared to use this moment to give the prospect insight into what you do and what's in it for them. This is where the rubber needs to meet the road: *why* you're calling and *what* they will get out of this unexpected and unplanned conversation have to come into alignment. (The Value Proposition Trifecta in the next section will help in defining and constructing what types of value can be delivered to cogently transmit your offering.)

The CP's *purpose* is singular. Our job is to now convert the conversation from a defensive posture to one that sparks interest in the prospect for what we offer. While "sparking interest" is a process behind a value statement, the value we deliver in this component will drive home what's in it for them. While the QP and the Hi whet the palate and even point out a pain, the CP is where impact is realized.

In fact, it could be said that everything in the cold call up to this point is a build-up to this moment. Recall from our discussion of the Trust Umbrella that one of the overall objectives of a cold call is to spark interest. So while there are other parts of the call that support this cause, this moment is where the flame stays on . . . or shuts off. So how do we spark interest? This will take some effort and refinement over time, but continuously analyzing your product relevance, your market, and the matching product-market fit will help the ideation of value for the audience you're reaching out to.

Lastly, the *instruction*.

There are two parts in the *instruction,* one building on the other. The first part is typically designed to help the prospect easily digest some basic mechanics of how the product or service works. This is so often overlooked, almost unequivocally, when I analyze and give feedback on clients' existing value propositions prior to translating them into our H2H method. The problem is we as salespeople perceive that our prospects want to hear advanced and highly technical or sophisticated features with optimal or maximum benefit *first*. While this feels right, it couldn't be further from the truth.

As we become more versed and advanced in our product, it is

easy for our minds to believe the world has been following our journey and can know the value we do. Such is human nature— our sense of self and awareness of others is a difficult separation. Applied to selling, our prospects' awareness of what we do is limited by and to their level of perception prior to our call, which to us is unknown. We can't bridge the gap by assuming they know where the bridge is or how to get across. We have to begin with the most basic of descriptions, giving us the highest chance of success that they will grasp the foundations before we build.

How is this done? By explaining the "how" and then working toward the "what." Here is an example:

Let's say we were at a work conference for a week together at an exotic location. However, I had visited this particular spot before. At one point during the week, I tell you and the others there is a waterfall nearby with warm, crystal-clear blue water, a place to swim safely, and a view of the local mountain ranges. I suggest we visit during some free time. In fact, I am convinced you have to see this view. I'm effervescing as I plead my case. I mean, it's a bucket-list-type of experience! Warm water, rays, beautiful view. Sounds like a cool way to relax after some long conference days, right? You can imagine yourself decompressing based on my description from the experience I've had before. You and the others are apprehensive though. Why not go? Especially after a long week indoors at a conference.

There is only one problem keeping you and the others from embarking on this epic journey: you can't see this "waterfall" from the lodge. We are surrounded by woods. There is also no accessible road to drive there. In fact, it's an hour walk to get there through the forest. Understandably, you're not so ready to commit to this "excursion" now, are you? It sounds more like a trip through Mordor with orcs and goblins along the path. "No thanks," you and the others say incredulously. "We'll just hang at the hotel pool where there aren't any dinosaurs or quicksand on the way there."

"Well, crap," I think to myself as I sulk. "How come no one wants to go?" I mumble to myself. "I described it just as I saw it when I visited before. How could they miss this view? Besides, we'll most likely never be able to experience this again together. It's also an easy walk there." I thought this was obvious. I continue ruminating: "In fact, there's a tour guide, bathrooms along the way, snack shacks, and the toe path is completely fenced in and patrolled by security" I say out loud, coming to as I was working through the logic. It hits me. "How could I be so thick!?" I smack my head with my palm. "I forgot to tell them this is a family-oriented, regularly visited, safe and secure journey to the falls!"

I run frantically to you and the others as fast as I can, as if I am trying to travel back in time to when I first pitched the idea to you. As I get to the lodge, out of breath, you and everyone else are walking out with backpacks, water shoes, and sunglasses on. "Where are you all headed?" I muster out while breathing hard.

"We're headed to your exotic destination! Thanks for the tip!"

"Wait, you are?" I question, scratching my head.

"Yeah! Great idea. The lifeguard at the hotel pool told us if we're going to come visit this area, we shouldn't spend it indoors swimming laps. Instead, we should walk to the end of the lot where there would be tour guides at the top of each hour walking us down to the waterfall. Are you coming along?"

I comply with ambivalence, happy we are going but shaking my head in disappointment that it took someone else to convince them to go.

What is the lesson here? Why didn't you and the others decide to go when I tried selling you on the dream? In fact, the lifeguard didn't seem to give much of a description of the waterfall. The only thing you and the others appeared to learn was that it was easy to get there! If people can't see the bridge, then why should they go across when they perceive danger? All of a sudden, risk, costs, time, and other factors come to the forefront. It's no longer about the features and benefits. It's now about what could go wrong. Quite the opposite of what we were trying to accomplish in the beginning, wasn't it?

This issue is very much a problem pervasive in all types of selling. We scream and shout with passion, waving our hands and jumping up and down hoping you join in. But all that is received is the view of a person acting crazy on the street corner. Why would anyone want to be screaming, shouting, and jumping around? Sounds like someone I may either want to run away from, or only confront if I think *they* need help. Whatever it is, I'm not buying what they are selling.

You've heard "Huge savings! Increase revenue! Save time!" These are all good and well, and can be very true. But the response to these familiar pitches are the same when we hear it like this first: "What's the catch?"

Sound familiar? This is the case far too often.

Salespeople who try to close too quickly start with poor messaging. Building trust is all about slow movement. Slow the process, speed the trust. The lesson is everywhere in selling, even in Calling Props.

Calling Props are all about ensuring there is a transition from idea to reality, and it is up to *you* as a salesperson to make the progressed connection. Whether in a cold call, an email, or sales presentation, selling propositions need to be built in the prospect's mind, not forced. A constant reminder I hear about selling propositions from just about every sales expert, author, or consultant out there in the sales improvement industry is never to "pitch slap," "word vomit," or even worse, make the proposition about the salesperson. The proposition is all about what's in it for the prospect. This includes every moment in our cold call. Yes, even this short conversation needs to be deconstructed and designed in words that are easy for the prospect to bridge the gap between dream and reality.

 STOP

Stop! This is a mission critical pause here! We just talked about the Calling Prop as our time to shine, highlight the value we provide, and tip the scale in our favor. This part of the conversation is crucial because, while the prospect is still skeptical, busy, or simply wants to end the conversation, you worked through the initial defenses in the QP and Hi and they are still on the phone!

The Calling Prop covers more than your product's features, benefits, and accolades. The CP is overarching, but it needs that special something that will make it really enticing. Enter The Value Proposition Trifecta (VPT): our careful construction of parts within your offering designed to spark your prospect's interest and encourage their belief in its ability to help their business. It's the model we use at H2H to take the ingredients in our CP recipe and prep them in such a way that they're tasty when cooked. The VPT is contained within your CP, and is the CP's main source of energy. The VPT will help the prospect take a bite by cooking up your CP to look good, smell good, and feel good!

Pausing now in our components section allows us to take a breath and focus on this crux in the conversation.

Ready?

VALUE PROPOSITION TRIFECTA (VPT)

Prior to reading this book, you may have heard common sales value words such as feature, benefit, and accolade. We have taken these ideas and developed a formula for extracting value from a company's offering and identifying what the possibilities are for the most poignant message in sparking interest with your prospect. Called The Value Proposition Trifecta, this is a means for delivering the most value to the prospect to drive and prove your product or service's efficacy more than at any other time in the conversation. The VPT supercharges these buzzwords and adds the precision and specificity required to render our message most salient when in conversation format.

The VPT is oriented around an offering's deliverables. When and if currency is exchanged for a product or service, the prospect should know its impacts prior to purchasing. The VPT aids in translating this impact. By adding advanced variations to common sales value terminology, offerings will almost always stand out better in our conversations and messaging. In short, the VPT supercharges impact. The three are:

- Differentiating Feature
- Tangible Benefit
- Outstanding Accolade

If the call is leading up to a moment, it's the opportunity to present the VPT. The moment of opportunity here is a window of attention and active listening from the client. This moment gives the cold caller power to influence and begin to believe you can help them. If you don't understand the true and most value you provide, how will the prospects know what's in it for them and have any reason for moving on to the next step with you? The VPT was designed to create organization around how to provide the most value. This way, when you're talking to your prospects, the value is easier for them to identify.

Let's dig into each value proposition key to understand how each one provides the most impact for your prospects.

1) Differentiating Feature

The first key is the *differentiating feature.* However, let's start out with a basic definition of a feature so we understand where the two diverge. In sales, a feature is a characteristic of a good or service that provides benefits to the consumer. The car is red, the marketing company creates websites, the insurance company provides specific insurance, the SaaS company has a web-based platform. Red, creates websites, provides specific insurance, and has a web-based platform are all features.

By contrast, the *differentiating feature* looks deeper into the offering to find something special about what the business *does.* We define the *differentiating feature* then as a fact or attribute about the offering that sets it apart or makes it unique in the marketplace. This carves a sharper definition streamlined for ultimate impact.

For example, if I were to say the car is red, it doesn't really make it too different, does it? Just about every car manufacturer has some type of red car! However, if I told you the red car has an electric engine (at least in 2020, when there weren't many), how much more differentiation is now at play versus other cars out there? The same goes for any business. For the marketing company, the basic feature was that they offer websites. However, the *differentiating feature* could be they specialize in creating websites specifically for Yoga studios. For the insurance company, maybe the insurance service doesn't just offer coverage, but it also offers educational consultations and unique reports for helping make better decisions which can reduce insurance costs even further. For the SaaS company, maybe the platform is the first of its kind in the industry. At SHP, the call team is 100% US-based and follows the only comprehensive cold call methodology publicly available from philosophy to frameworks designed for setting sales appointments and leads (H2H!). Now, this might not seem like it's a feature of the offering, but for us at SHP, we sell people skills. So when our prospects hear this, it helps give them confidence and builds trust because it's not traditional for what an outsourced telemarketing or sales development company typically provides as part of its features.

Applied to cold phone calling, providing value fast requires thought, strategy, and preparedness to convert these conversations with decision makers most effectively and efficiently. This is where the *differentiating features* can spark interest and illuminate new ideas and applications to the prospects' business they may not have considered or did not know existed prior to your call.

2) Tangible Benefit

The second key is the *tangible benefit*. Again, before we define the *tangible benefit*, let's define the root word. A benefit can be defined as the value delivered to the prospect via the features of a product or service. The car is red so it appears desirable by others. The marketing company creates websites so potential customers can find businesses, which can then sell more. The insurance company provides specific insurance for top coverage and low rates; the SaaS company has a web-based directory to connect consumers to businesses more quickly.

The *tangible benefit,* like the *differentiating feature,* increases the impact of the benefit, creating a higher chance of sparking interest with the prospect to move them to Next Steps (the final component we'll discuss after the VPT!). Increasing the impact in a cold phone call takes specificity and/or measurement, hence the name "tangible." We define the *tangible benefit* as a form of value, results, or type of impact to the prospect's business that is measurable.

Out of the three, I have the most fun discovering and delivering this one! There are so many pitches, value propositions, and scripts that get *so close* to providing a real measurable benefit. The problem? They don't quite word it right, and it doesn't have as much impact.

My favorite example: Let's just say the business I worked for had really good customer service. If I were to tell you, "You're really going to love the customer service here. It's great. It's fantastic customer service. You're going to have a really good experience." Is that really measurable? Not that I see! There is nothing but fluff and adjectives in that description of the benefit. Remember our H2H Characteristics? It's better to choose action verbs over adjectives in our language.

If I were to make this a tangible benefit, the value still being you're going to receive customer service, the tangible benefit would be something like this, "So [decision maker], what's unique about our customer service is we'll respond within 60 minutes of any inquiry." There it is. That is a tangible benefit! Why? First of all, I used a number to describe what the value was going to be. This way, it's instantly easier for the prospect to understand how it's going to impact them? Now the prospect can think to themself, "Oh, okay. Yeah. If I have any issue or anything, I know I can hear back within 60 minutes." I also didn't use a lot of the fluff I talked about. I used action verbs. What's unique about our customer service is that we will get back to you within 60 minutes. I'm describing with good bones and providing a measurable result.

Here's another example: At SHP, an example might be, "We can increase lead flow at your company by 1-to-100 leads per month depending on the market and package you choose." Now, that's pretty tangible, isn't it? I listed exactly the number of leads they could potentially expect if they were to use our service. What if I were to just say, "Hey, yeah, we can help grow your business, and you're going to get all sorts of leads, it's going to be great?" Well, sure, this sounds nice, but unless I have something tangible, it's going to be hard for the decision maker to wrap their mind around the correct interpretation of the type of value I can provide. Using our red car example, if I were to say the electric red car reduces the car owner's fuel bill by 95% per month, that's much different than just saying we can help reduce fuel costs. See the difference? The same goes for any business.

Let's continue with some prior examples to identify some strong *tangible benefits:*

- The marketing company specializes in creating websites specifically for Yoga studios, *increasing audience web traffic by 50%*.
- The insurance company offers educational consultations and unique reports *to reduce your premium by up to 25%*.
- The SaaS company's web-based directory connects consumers to businesses more quickly, *increasing sales for registered businesses up to 75%* compared to those without it.

For your offering, what discovery work do you need to do to identify measurable benefits? Do you measure them regularly so that it's simply a matter of applying them to your messaging as a sales tool? Do you need to design an initial testing phase and measure the outcomes for the first time? Or, does your team need to work on your product a bit more so it can produce sustained and measurable success?

Tangible benefits are better to have for your prospects but require more work. While this can sound daunting, the silver lining is that more work equals easier connection with prospects. Continuous improvement is a business best practice needed to provide customers with better and better results. If this is already your company's model, you shouldn't have any problem regularly identifying and measuring tangible benefits.

3) Outstanding Accolade

The third and final key is the *outstanding accolade*. This VPT key is different from the first two in that the *differentiating feature* and *tangible benefit* work together hand in hand. To learn the *outstanding accolade* and how it applies, then, let's look at the basic definition of an accolade before delving further. An accolade can be defined as a form of praise or recognition attributed to your business from positive experiences or results realized. Basic accolades can include:

- A positive written review from a customer
- A customer experience video testimonial
- A base number of customers served
- A mention in a local news article or blog
- The owner or figurehead in the business has notoriety

Simply put, the accolade shows credibility. For example, the web design business has *several 5-star reviews on Google*. Or, the business was *featured in the local news as a rising star in the insurance space*. These basic accolades act as a prerequisite to the outstanding accolade. At the end of the day, the question buzzing in your prospect's mind that you want to answer is, "Does this company know what it's doing?" Answering that question comes from accolades and proof in the pudding.

Transitioning to *outstanding* is a process by which the accolades earned become rare, high-ranking, high-performing, or recommended by significant, reputable sources.

The *outstanding accolade* is defined as a ranking, accomplishment, or referral that sets a business apart in the marketplace. Think of an accolade as the first stripes earned, and the *outstanding accolade* as the proven track record of success crowning the business a player in bigger leagues. If an accolade shows credibility, the *outstanding accolade* conveys the business, at least perceivably, is at a higher level of authority in the space.

For instance, at SHP, where we serve business sizes from small to mid to large, one of our first outstanding accolades was an accomplishment of serving 500 businesses across the globe. Or the fact we've served major companies such as AmerisourceBergen, Uber, Moen, *The Economist*, and most recently, Amazon. Another could be when we made the United States Inc. 5000 list.

The *outstanding accolade* answers important questions, such as "Is this company the best option for my business?" "Does this company deserve my investment more than the others I'm considering?" Or "Have they done excellent work for my industry or businesses like mine?"

Credibility and track record can range from company to company and industry to industry. But no matter the stage, accolades are essential for establishing credibility with potential clients. Identifying and utilizing one or more of these in cold phone calls enables trust to be built more quickly.

Now that we have learned and identified all three value proposition keys, we can begin to consider what they might look like in a script. Which do we say first? Do we say them all at once? What if we don't have them all defined?

The idea is to have a basic "how" statement listed in your Calling Prop, but then work towards using bullets to separate the type of value so you can adjust and adapt to what the conversation requires. If we look back at the CP for SHP, you can now see the VPT in the Calling Prop here:

...so the way it works is we help companies generate leads and appointments for their sales pipeline by making outbound calls and emails to their prospects through campaigns on a month-to-month basis.

- *Differentiating Feature: We have US-based sales development reps that work for you using the only comprehensive cold call method available from philosophy to frameworks.*
- *Tangible Benefit: We typically generate between 1 to 100 leads per month for our clients depending on the project size and industry*
- *Outstanding Accolade: We have done work for hundreds of SMBs up to companies such as AmerisourceBergen, Moen, Uber, and Amazon*

The creation of these VPT keys for a business offering can seem daunting. If you are creating your script for the first time, or looking to improve upon the one you have, you may feel naked realizing your features, benefits, or accolades don't quite have the additional spices the VPT adds. And this is okay! It is normal not to have any or all defined. The goal is to look at what makes the ultimate combination of value. For every business, there is value to be delivered. Just like every person is different and unique, every business can be the same. We just have to find what makes it unique. If you're having trouble, the point is to identify a distinct value you can easily define, and build from there as your business grows. As time goes on, the other VPT keys will become clear as you work with your team to identify, develop, or establish them. And start small. An easy example to apply is if you are working in a competitive space, adding "local to" or "specialized in" in an industry are very easy pivots for your VPT that can build trust with prospects more quickly. For smaller businesses, the differentiating feature is traditionally easier because there is usually something unique or special about the product or service itself you can speak to. Small-to-midsize businesses seem to lean into the tangible benefits, while enterprise-level businesses who have heavy competition tend to lean more into their outstanding accolades. The VPT is not one-size-fits-all. But since we only have a few short minutes to speak with prospects, consistently reviewing and refining our VPT over time will only sharpen the proposition and enable us to convert higher as we progress.

Discovery Q's

There are two optional, albeit highly recommended subcomponents in the CCF that can significantly impact the buy-in, belief, and show rates of cold calls. The reason they are "recommended" or "optional" rather than required are because they follow a critical point in the call which is difficult to control. In other words, after the CP, and even the Hi in some situations, the conversation can take many turns outside of what is prescribed in the script.

Let me just say that *this can be a good thing*. Requiring rigid steps in any script turns it into something more like a theatrical performance (wherein both "actors" recite "lines") rather than a purposeful, yet free-flowing dialogue between two humans, seller and a buyer. *Discovery Q's*, or discovery questions, are open-ended questions asked after the CP that are designed to keep the prospect engaged while the you learn more about how receptive the prospect is to the conversation, their use case and familiarity with the product or service being offered, and any additional feelings and pains they may be experiencing.

Additionally, keep in mind that the rule of reciprocity doesn't stop at the Hone-in. Any opportunity (especially ones that are the result of natural law) that causes the prospect to feel they owe us a chance to respond can tee up our final component, the NXTS, or next steps, extremely well.

Discovery Q's need to be strategic and open-ended but also require forethought on the part of the salesperson calling. Unlike the Hi, the *Discovery Q's* can go into uncharted territory, alternately prompting feelings and thoughts the prospect may have been waiting to get off their chest to someone like you on one hand, or short and/or easy answers for you to deal with on the other. Either way, at this juncture in the conversation, you are looking to close out this initial conversation and move on to your next step. To get there, remember that many of the responses a prospect discloses are generally easier to harness into the kind of NXTS answer that can increase your chances for the meeting or primary next-step objective you're looking for.

Here are some recommended *Discovery Q's* you can adopt or adapt based on your offering type and target prospect:

- What solutions are you using now?
- What strategies have worked for you?
- What problems have you had in the past managing this area?
- What would be an ideal state for you in this department?

There are plenty more possibilities, and they may need to be adjusted based on your offering and market combination. But all these questions share an important quality: they are all open-ended questions. Sounds a bit counterintuitive right? Especially after we said to use a *balanced question* in the Hone-in. It can make sense to use these *Discovery Q's*, but it's crucial early on to stay on track while building trust quickly.

As we've discussed, using a *balanced question* gives the caller a higher chance of control in moving the conversation forward towards more rapport and relationship-building. If the conversation has reached this point, however, we have seen openness and candor give way to more connection, which might even segway into a NXTS tee-up. See, we have already given our pitch through the CP. The prospect knows what we can do and how we can help. At this crossroads, we are in transition to asking for a commitment in the NXTS. The prospect is beginning to consider if this offering can work for them, or at least considering why it would not. We accept this; at a minimum, it shows us that their mind has shifted to the topic we came to discuss. It's too early to tell if our offering is a good fit in their mind, so the best we can do is begin the conversation—which is the essence of a cold call.

At this point, open-ended questions aren't dangerous anymore. Rather, they unlock the next component: the NXTS. Remember, our Trust Umbrella lists one of the objectives of a call as "sell the NXTS" rather than the product or service itself. By asking a *Discovery Q*, we anticipate the conversation will tee up a final question once we actively listen, take notes, and allow the rule of reciprocity to work its magic.

Extended Prop

The second and final optional sub-component of the CCF is the *Extended Prop*. This component is truly optional—in fact, it may not even be needed in many conversations. In others, though, it can be essential.

We use a rule of thumb for cold callers that states every caller should be prepared with a minimum of two pieces of value ready for use. This means that while it is natural for us to be prepared with a feature, benefit, or accolade to help describe more about how we can help them, it's best to have another backup value piece ready to go. While it is not expected of SDRs to know products and services from soup to nuts, having enough information to spark interest is essential. This standard is based on our *primary objectives* mentioned in the Trust Umbrella. While there may be differing opinions about how much a sales development rep should divulge, The H2H Method™ for Cold Calling states it is not the job of the person calling, whether they are the one taking the next meeting or not, to fully deploy a professional sales presentation here (in fact, a sales presentation shouldn't happen on the first call with someone, anyway). Too much information is overload and could cut short the opportunity to meet the goals of our cold call (spark interest, diffuse the *salesperson stigma,* and sell the *next step*). Too little could sound as if you are incompetent and wasting the prospect's time without transferring the proper knowledge and belief.

Since much of our language is based around sales statements and questions, some prospects may catch on that you don't have any real information that can help them. They may call you out and leave you feeling and looking like a deer in headlights. The *Extended Prop* gives you, as the caller or SDR, the additional product expertise to back up the offering descriptions and value statements you so confidently deployed early on in the call.

Below are some examples of additional value statements that could be added for SHP:

- *We can build lists for you monthly if you don't have access to data*
- *We have the only fully comprehensive trademarked and copyrighted cold call methodology covering philosophy to frameworks*
- *Our appointment-setting rate average is over 1% and ranges from 0.25% to 12% on the number of dials we make, depending on industry. This is 1 appointment every 400 calls to 1 appointment every 8 or so calls*
- *Each client is assigned an account manager. These team members act as your outsourced sales manager*
- *We offer some of the lowest-priced entry-level packages with US-based client SDRs*
- *We have written over 2000 custom scripts for over 50 industry origins and to 50 industries targets*
- *We have clients who have been with us for more than 4 years*

NXTS - NEXT STEPS

The final stage in the CCF is the NXTS. The next steps wrap up the work we so diligently executed into an identifiable action item for you and your prospect. Remember, these are "next steps." The next-step philosophy is identifying what action can be taken by the end of the conversation to move our new business relationship towards a partnership. However, there is a distinction about what the NXTS is designed to accomplish.

NXTS | Next Steps

- **(A)ssumptions**
  - High probability of interest if first three components completed
- **(P)urpose**
  - Identify & agree on next steps
- **(I)nstruction**
  - Always ask for next step in accordance to strategy prior to call

As I've already stated, *first cold call outbound touches to potential customers virtually never turn into a sale on the same call.* It may seem that I'm belaboring the point here, but I assure you that in my script-writing and outbound work over the last 10 years, I have yet to see it happen. And yet, sales professionals in twenty-first-century selling, especially in the B2B marketplace, routinely accept this utter impossibility as their goal.

The effective method in the twenty-first century, then, is to sell the next step in the sales process, not the product or service itself yet. Unfortunately, Modern Sales Failure is all too real, virtually resulting in prospect PTSD. Prospect reactions and responses can be illogical or irrational based on our requests for next steps. But respecting these feelings and reactions by displaying empathy, actively listening, and verbally confirming their feelings, builds trust on the grounds of shared understanding. By relying on the H2H purpose—building that trust—we diffuse the stigma prospects feel about the sales appointment or meeting and build more trust, more quickly. As we've discussed, it's a phenomenon in which we can actually speed the sales process back up by doing so.

Let me say that again. Prospects often feel flight or fight about sales people. They feel they are being sold at a time when they aren't ready or may not know yet if they want what is being sold to them. They feel the pressure to have their credit card or check ready to sign and pay when confronted by a salesperson. By guiding the conversation away from a sale and towards education, the caller can help the prospect recover from the stigma, lower their defenses, and begin trusting the salesperson.

But while a cold call to introduce and inform about a product only may be the easiest and most effective way to fully diffuse the stigma, sales won't be made in any form if some type of next steps aren't identified. The objective in creating and identifying the best NXTS for your company is to balance the natural buying cycle of prospects in your industry with sensible selling cycles found for the offering you are presenting.

There is a wide range of suitable NXTS depending on the company, and there is also just as large a discussion around what NXTS should be as best practice in professional selling. We've seen NXTS range from permission to send an email, mail, or fax to on-the-spot website registrations or surveys to appointment meetings to permission to send info and initiate a follow-up call, and more. For many companies, the sales "appointment" or "meeting" is the most commonly accepted NXTS, typically implemented by sales management as an easier way to tag base-level commitment along the sales cycle. In addition, it's typically perceived as a satisfiable and achievable goal for sales professionals to reach while conducting outreach and initiating movement along the company sales pipeline to meet targets.

At SHP, there are four basic NXTS Tiers customizable by companies based on strategy, objective, and need: *appointment lead, survey lead, warm lead, and nurture lead.* Each has its own set of rules so that the cold caller can walk through the options that best fit the prospect's comfort level with the request. This way, while highest NXTS are attempted, lower grades of prospect commitment are accepted. These are considered play-by-play tiers.

Think of an *appointment lead* of higher value in the sales cycle than a warm by nature, and a *warm lead* a higher value than a *nurture lead* (we'll define each of these in detail momentarily). However, it doesn't always translate. SHP asks client SDRs to provide notes for each lead set, acting as "color commentary" to what happened on the call with the prospect. In some cases, the NXTS is simply the most comfortable or suitable way for a prospect to interact. For instance, in basketball a 3-point shot in the first quarter is valuable, but a 1-point free throw to win the game could be the most priority play that day. Valuing *nurture, warm,* and *appointment leads* communicates to prospects that their buying cycle is more important than the sales cycle placed on them.

Keep this play-by-play and color commentary theme in mind as we define each lead. While one "play-by-play" may seem worth more than another, the color commentary from the conversation can tell a different story. Both are important, so be mindful, and remember that the idea is to *not* judge the customer. After all, they were just called out of the blue. What I mean is just because someone may only commit to receiving some information without explicit permission to call back, let alone set an appointment time, it doesn't mean they aren't interested. Similarly, just because someone expresses interest right away and sets an appointment, doesn't mean they purchase, let alone show up!

Treat every lead equally as important as the next, even if there is natural priority commitment to higher-tiered leads. For instance, we frequently cold call people who answer their phone on vacation! It is not uncommon for these prospects to be interested in the solution we are presenting, but they don't want to set a meeting or commit to anything until they receive collateral on the product or service. In fact, we have received reports of these types of calls turning into sales later on!

Here are the definitions of the four primary NXTS tiers utilized at SHP. They may or may not fit your business and sales-funnel steps exactly, but understand they're meant to help you make order out of ostensible chaos.

An *appointment lead*, as defined by SHP, is a positive decision maker or stakeholder conversation resulting in an agreed-upon meeting at a later date and time. It would also need to be clear on the part of both parties that the purpose of the meeting is to further discuss the product or service offered on the first cold, voice-to-voice conversation. Once set by the cold caller, these meetings are typically held with either the person calling or with another team member such as an account executive. This can be held in a number of ways, and the choice of appointment medium can vary greatly depending on the company's sales process, industry targeted, or person reached. Appointment meetings can be held via phone call, web conference, in-person, or other environments where live, voice-to-voice exchange can occur. An appointment meeting would not typically be counted as such if the exchange would be via text.

A *survey lead* would be considered at a similar level to an *appointment lead*. The reason is because it could be identified as a pre-discovery call with certain checkpoints that need to be met before it is considered qualified. An introduction is given, light value is provided, followed by a list of questions around the purpose of qualifying or gathering opinions. The length and depth of the conversation gives weight to the commitment from both sides, deeming these highest-level NXTS, in most cases.

The second level of interest based on the SHP NXTS tier rules is a *warm lead*. This is when a prospect has given the SDR permission to follow up with a call, just not at a specific date and time. A lot of times this is somebody who might have a busy schedule, is a little bit tentative on their commitment, and/or wants to receive some information first to learn a little bit more. What separates a *warm lead* from an *appointment lead* is that the prospect has explicitly stated they would not commit to a specific date and time to meet for an in-person meeting, web conference, or discovery call.

NOTE: *Further, to clarify gray areas, SHP client SDRs are prohibited from setting up appointment meetings as "follow-up calls." Remember, the goal isn't just to set an appointment, but to set it in a way that sparks enough interest for them to show up. The data shows cold calls using the terms "follow-up call" or "call back" have a lower chance of the prospect turning up to them. Internally, if this word is used, the call is automatically dropped to a warm lead status. Whether you are selling a single product or work for multiple compa-*

nies cold calling, treat this term as taboo unless it truly is simple
permission to call again with little commitment.

The last traditional play-by-play NXTS tier is a *nurture lead*. A *nurture lead* is different from most other NXTS because, while it is permission given by the prospect to receive information, it is *without* explicit permission to call again. Color commentary here can range, but just like in any other NXTS tier, it is important for the sales pipeline. As aforementioned, *nurture leads* can turn into *appointment leads*, proposals, and sales. While they may not always be prioritized over first-time set appointments, they are qualified enough to send educational material, connect on social media, add to email sequences, and individually follow up on how your product or service may serve them.

The NXTS API is framed with the range of lead definition tiers. Regardless of the play-by-play ask, there is an *assumption, purpose,* and *instruction* just like the other components. The *assumption* suggests there is a high probability of some level of interest if the first three components are completed in the conversation, and the NXTS is reached. As we'll discuss in the Conversion Probability Timeline, the longer a conversation goes, the higher probability there will be for some type of quality next action committed by the prospect. Assuming there is a high chance of conversion to at least one of the play-by-play tiers, the ensuing *purpose* and *instruction* then is to identify and agree on next steps. This is done by asking for an appointment, follow-up call (*warm lead*), or permission to send info (*nurture*). The options give the cold caller ways to meet the prospect where they are in their buying cycle. so you can move them down your sales funnel while maintaining trust in the person, product, and process.

The grand idea behind the NXTS tiers may not be obvious from the outset, but the philosophy is built into the framework. H2H is achieved in cold calling when high-performance opportunities are maximized without ever losing trust with prospects. By design, we aim for higher-priority appointments or surveys, adapting to lower-priority, albeit still-important, warm and nurture grades of request when it makes sense. By creating systems, mechanisms, and labels for meeting prospects where they are along their buying cycle, the pressure is off the highest priority ask of an appointment only, diffusing the *salesperson stigma* even more.

Especially in old-school and outdated sales philosophies of cold calling, aggressive management techniques many times enforce appointment-only results, preaching rhetoric about not giving up until an appointment is set. In some settings, sales representatives aren't "paid unless an appointment is made." In fact, many outsourced sales development companies sell by "the appointment," forcing pressure on both the prospector and the prospect to meet, even if it doesn't make the most sense. While designing agreements, employment roles, systems, and compensation around appointment results isn't inherently evil and can work —the system creates a strain on its people by prioritizing results over good process, diminishing quality and motivation.

Cold calling, as mentioned in our belief statement, can work 100% of the time if people pick up the phone and the particular product is relevant, but it is a never-ending process of improvement. Good process equals good results, and at a cost of no trust left behind.

> NOTE: *This fundamentally opens up another can of worms I won't spend too much time on in this book, but it is related and worth mentioning. SHP has never offered "by appointment" pricing to this point. Never say never, but that approach is fundamentally against our H2H method philosophy of "maximizing high performance without ever losing trust with prospects" and principally against good sales development. The amount of times I get asked if we offer this still is beyond me. Not only does "appointment only" pricing place undue pressure on SDRs, the same pressure is placed on prospects. In the unlearning of outdated and aggressive sales techniques, this impedes progress. Instead, the value needs to be placed on the prioritization of interest levels and lead types. This level of service enables prospects to build trust with prospects, while companies create new funnels and systems for*

engaging at the pace and timing the prospect is ready for—it's a win-win.

Example Appointment Setting Script

Here is an example of the NXTS cold phone call appointment setting script with all three NXTS tier options as backup:

The reason I'm calling is to see if you would be available for a [NXTS HIGHEST TIER APPOINTMENT REQUEST] to see if this is something that would work or make sense for you. Would you be open to this?

If yes to highest NXTS Tier appointment request

[Go to 4.B HOUSEKEEPING]

If no to highest NXTS Tier appointment request

[START WITH EMAIL]. No problem. Would you be open to an email to learn a little more about how this can help?

If yes to lower NXTS Tier

[NURTURE ATTEMPT] Okay, we will send. What is your email address? [COLLECT EMAIL]

[WARM LEAD/APPT ATTEMPT 2] Once you've had some time to review, would a quick call to see your thoughts on if we could help work for you?

Let's break down the script example piece by piece. Some cold call advice I see suggests "the reason" for the call should be stated earlier in the conversation. I wouldn't say "never" when suggesting when to use "the reason," but I would say to save it as long as possible until the best moment.

Explaining our reason is a reflection of our intention. In no way are we attempting to deceive a prospect by holding back, but if we state the reason for our call early in the conversation, it can weigh down a part of the conversation in unproductive ways, or be untruthful to my final intention. For example, if I were to add my reason to the Hone-in, such as "The reason for my call is to see if you have an outsourced, lead-generation partner . . ." then I am placing the weight on something which isn't true to my final intention.

I have caught myself stating the reason early from time to time.

It's not always a game changer, but why do we do this? Prematurely stating the reason usually happens because of fear or disbelief in the value of your offer and lack of confidence in your delivery. In other words, we say it early because it makes us feel better. It's a crutch.

Let's take it a step further. If I were to make a cold call to a prospect, focus the reason for my call on the Hone-in, and expect them to provide the answer, the prospect may be confused as to why they need to spend time or participate if they have already given me my reason for calling when asking for the meeting later in the NXTS component stage. In fact, their head could be clouded with "Oh, so they want me on an appointment with them to sell me. This is the *true* reason for their call." Placing "the reason" for our call at the right place ensures the prospect can focus on the product, its value, and never have to worry about sly sales tricks.

I have found those prospect conversations best suited for using the CCF are most successful when I match the energy and word placement throughout my conversations. Doing so creates a dialogue around the logic of our call structure. Combining words matched with emotional attunement provides a powerful, belief-based delivery to our prospects. Asking the prospect directly for your request and giving them the reason during the NXTS establishes expectations and the goal, giving you clarity as to why they wouldn't move towards the next step if they deny your request. (The Objections and Responses section covers this.)

Asking specifically for what you need in order to help your prospect strengthens the relationship in other ways: it shows assertiveness and leadership by guiding your prospect to the next natural step in your sales pipeline.

If we receive a "yes" to the appointment-ask, congratulations! However, your work is not done! While it is easy to get excited here, maintaining composure is imperative. Showing unmatched excitement to a prospect who has accepted your request may cause them to back off. Remember, this is the first time we have met. The more we can communicate a neutral or mirrored approach in our delivery at this moment, the more we can extract sales stigma out of the call.

On the other hand, if we don't get a "yes" to the meeting, we can back into asking permission to send information and follow up-call, (*warm lead*), or even revert to permission to send email (nurture). While these aren't ideal for our sales pipeline, they are essential for sustaining trust when prospects aren't ready. Further, the leads in these tiers have real potential to turn to higher NXTS play-by-play levels anyway.

The amount of stories we hear about *nurture leads* converting to signed deals for SHP clients sometimes overpowers the internal appointment news channels. Crowds and clients roar in celebration, as if it was an epic comeback win in the final minutes of a championship game. But why? Simply put, it showcases the power in sustaining business relationships until it's the best time for the buyer. When the cold caller works their best to maximize results for their company, while never losing trust with the prospect, it conveys the painstaking work done to weave an aggressive sales cycle with a delicate buying cycle.

The NXTS component moves potential energy to kinetic energy with the prospect. The product and service has stored impact, and the NXTS tiers spark the process to deliver. Without the NXTS, there is little to no tangible control over the outbound sales development pipeline, rendering the use of the call to unpredictable inbound call-back potential, costing the seller and the seller's company time and money in an effort to earn ROI on the outbound efforts. Businesses must earn money. As billionaire businessman Mark Cuban says in his book *How to Win at the Sport of Business*, "Sales cures all."[2] If cold calling isn't generating opportunity at some point, then inevitably there won't be investment cold calling at all. The H2H Method™ supports sales performance, respects the ask, and demands results, but its ideals never sacrifice a business relationship.

Housekeeping & Qualifying Questions

Let's say that we have gone through the entire CCF script with a targeted contact. We delivered the QP, asked the opening Hi question, went through the Bridge Statement, provided value in our CP, asked a few other Discovery Qs, and ended with a close and a commitment to a date and time with our new prospect. Congratulations! The hardest parts are done. But, in our excitement, we forget about the details. The email address wound up with an extra "n." The time zone is one hour ahead, and the first and last names are different from traditional spellings. The prospect doesn't receive the email because it's addressed to a different name, and anyway, the meeting is at the wrong time. Not only does additional work have to be done and time spent to get this information correct, but if we don't do damage control early, the prospect could be gone faster than my first dates from Hinge.

Fortunately, Housekeeping & Qualifying Questions subcomponents help tighten the details and prepare the prospect for the next steps ahead. The reason this is tough is because in cold calling, our successes are based on the belief transference of a product's value relevance from salesperson to value receiver. If these people were reaching out to us first, they would be the ones who already have shown a level of belief the product or service might work, easing the friction in initial business communication efforts between the buyer and the seller. In initial cold outreach, as discussed in the BRT, cold calling is the only instance in business relationships where the contact does not have an established relationship with us of any sort. This chasm between outbound and inbound creates a unique lens for the seller through which to view prospects.

Wait—why am I talking about cold calling again philosophically in the Housekeeping & Qualifying Questions section? Because the cleanup at the end of a call is distinctly important in keeping initially successful cold calls just that—successful—through the next significant interaction (i.e., a sales appointment). In traditional cold calling where there was no indication someone could use the product or service being offered, prospects may not have considered anything like what we are offering prior to our call. However, this is where salespeople come in! This is our role. Our job is to disrupt their current process, to help them understand something they may have not known prior. The challenge is the outbound lead chase can sometimes feel a bit different than working inbound leads. The difference is rooted in the fact that prior to the moment an inbound lead reaches out to us, they have already established a PIN (pain, interest, or need). They have started looking for solutions, researched you in some aspect before calling, and made a call with a typical buying time frame already in mind. They have already thought about the process, and you as a seller are part of it.

Conversely, in cold calling there may be a chance we catch someone along that timeline, but in many industry cases, we don't. In most cold call conversation scenarios, we're initiating conversation, sparking thought-provoking actions, and identifying next steps to move them along. This is not an easy task, and it's up to us as cold callers to continue the connection and transfer belief. The misconception is that once we hear curiosity or interest on a cold call, we can easily start to envision signed contracts and commission checks. However, unless we have been trained in the proper follow-up, our instincts after a cold call can unintentionally be far from the best follow-up process steps. Since we can become excited from the outcome, we think that excitement is translated to the same commitment by the prospect. We don't follow up, don't connect on LinkedIn, don't send reminders, and we wonder why they don't show up to the appointment or respond down the road. If best practice steps aren't followed here, many of our cold calls will go to waste, which is not something we can afford in a one-on-one interaction channel.

Driving home the follow-up details gives us a glimpse into why housekeeping and qualifying questions help solidify and tighten the initial connection between buyer and seller. The belief needs to turn into action, instead of dissipating. We do this by remembering to button up our details and ask the right questions to help solidify our next call.

The image below reflects the design of the H2H Housekeeping & Qualifying Questions section of the script:

4.B HOUSEKEEPING (Use applicable steps depending on NXTS tier agreed upon)

Okay, great.

1. How is [DATE] at [TIME]?

[WORK TO OFFER NEW TIMES IF FIRST DOESN'T WORK]

2. What is your email address so I can make sure you receive the invite?

3. And just to confirm, your email is [SPELL OUT EMAIL ADDRESS]?

4. And you spell your name [SPELL OUT BASED ON YOUR DATA, OR, ASK HOW TO SPELL IF YOU JUST RECEIVED THEIR NAME FOR FIRST TIME]?

5. [IF POSSIBLE, SEND A CALENDAR INVITE VIA YOUR CALENDAR SCHEDULER LINK (IE, CALENDLY.COM, HUBSPOT SCHEDULER, BOOKME SCHEDULER, ETC.) BEFORE CLOSING OUT THE CALL AND CONFIRM WITH THEM THEY RECEIVED IT]

And just before we end the call, I have a couple quick questions to ask to prepare how we can help you!

[Go to 4.C QUALIFYING QUESTIONS]

4.C Qualifying Questions Post NXTS:

1) How many leads do you need per week or month to hit your goals?
2) What kind of outbound lead generation strategies have you done in the past?

Thank you, and looking forward to meeting on [DATE] at [TIME]!

The Housekeeping step comes before the Qualifying Questions. Housekeeping is designed to identify exact and specific information critical for tying up the loose pieces of communication data. Qualifying Questions then are questions designed to gather objective or subjective information from the prospect for two reasons:

1. Objective information—such as number of employees, users, desks with computers, or leads needed per week, etc. can help the selling company:

a.) Quantify if the prospect has the minimal resources necessary for the selling company's return to be worth the investment in servicing the potential customer

b.) Prepare proper slides, math, resources, and case studies relevant to the potential customer's pains, interests, or needs come time for the appointment or selling discussion

2. Subjective information—such as current strategies, plans, opinions, and feedback to:

a.) Draw out more committed thought from the prospect by asking questions that provoke awareness, self-analysis, or evaluation of their state with the product or service in discussion

b.) Gather opinions and fodder to prepare slides, math, resources, stories, and case studies relevant to the potential customer's pains, interests, needs and subjective answers come time for the appointment or selling discussion

There are schools of thought around asking the Qualifying Questions early in the conversation. While this can sometimes create allure, the issues are:

1. Conversation becomes about you as the seller
2. Not enough trust built in early stages. Prospects can feel they are giving away information at an unknown and dangerous expense.

In the Survey Script Format, this form of questioning can work, but trust and familiarity must be gained, and quickly, if information is to be divulged freely by the prospect.

Housekeeping and Qualifying Questions give credence to a cold call. While an appointment or interest may seemingly be gained, this step enables both sides to pause and reflect to ensure commitment and next steps are true and sincere. They add nothing but quality to a conversation if followed well, and are crucial steps rarely discussed amongst cold callers.

Conversion Probability Timeline

In the CCF, there is enough data from our calls made at SHP using this framework to suggest that as time in a cold phone call increases, so do the odds of converting a conversation to *quality* next steps. Moving from left to right, you see the QP, Hi, CP, and NXTS. The order of the components demonstrates a natural human sales conversation progression with a prospect that illustrates the likelihood of a desired next step, which is identified as time increases. As seen in the Conversion Probability Timeline image, the ball starts to roll into your court once you have gotten past the QP and the Hi. The scale is now tipping in your favor towards a quality conversation filled with prospect interest. It is your time to shine!

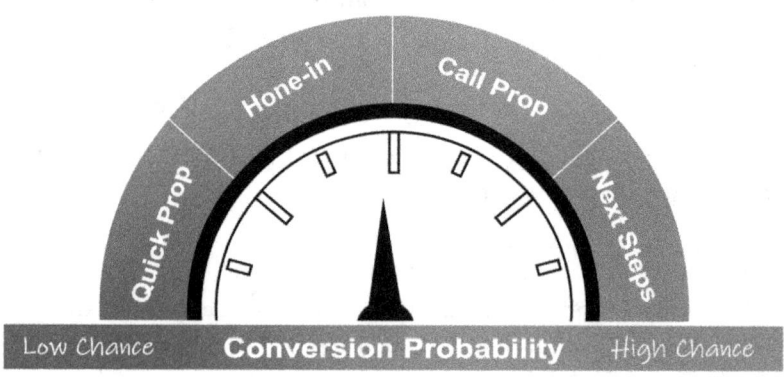

The Conversion Probability Timeline is designed to provide a visualization of how our chances increase throughout the call in the CCF. As discussed, the first two components in the CCF act as defensive moves. Assuming that prospects experience the *salesperson stigma* in the first few seconds of a conversation, we as SDRs are already in a hole. In order to dig our way out, simply getting through the first few seconds is our goal. Overcompensating, trying too hard, and word vomiting can backfire, sending us quickly to a dial tone. Knowing the likelihood of conversion is low in the first few seconds helps us realize how fragile cold phone conversations really are. The better we can get through those first few moments, the more we'll earn more opportunities to lengthen the conversation, increasing the probability of NXTS conversion.

To break it down even further, the Quick Prop and Hone-in are the defensive parts of the conversation. Truly, our purpose as discussed in the QP and Hi APIs, is really to not get hung up on. However, once you start to move to the center of the conversation and into the Calling Prop, the ball starts to roll into your court. As time goes on, you gain more control of the result of the call, and the longer we can continue the conversation, the better chance we have of converting those next steps that we're looking for. The better we can fully grasp our purpose in these moments, the better we become at managing ourselves & performing through these crucial moments.

The Calling Prop stage is where we have the opportunity to deliver the greatest amount of features, benefits, and accolades that can resonate the most with prospects. It's where, if delivered well by the caller, the prospect can begin to see impact for their business. As we move here and perform well with a strong *value proposition trifecta (VPT)*, the chances of success increase. This is where top performers live—in the CP, Discovery Questions *(subcomponent)*, and in the NXTS. The more we can live here with prospects, the higher our conversion will be during cold phone calls with decision makers.

Using this visualization can help remind us that every second matters. As you go further, your chances increase and enable you to hold on longer when/if the conversation feels like you're losing control. Sticking with it and aligning yourself with each component can give you the best chance for success to convert quality next steps with your prospect.

CHAPTER 23
THE NO-BULL SCRIPT

Sometimes, the CCF isn't the most conducive for highest conversion in every market. Even though the CCF is typically the script framework we default to in many B2B markets, we have found it doesn't always prove to be the best for specific industries or particular *target client personas* (TCP).

For instance, in marketplaces highly saturated with SDR calls, we've found there can be a more heavily weighted stigma that creates a subconscious and instinctive negative reaction to sales calls. One example is in the commercial insurance industry, where there's a heavy presence of insurance salespeople and insurance offerings reaching targeted companies to offer a lower rate or better coverage.

In these situations, it can be more advantageous to add value to the QP in our introduction. Even though there is inherent risk in delivering too much, too early, and for too long, it can be easier for the receiving end to digest and process before they feel it's just another sales call. If you can speak to them more fully while they are actively listening in the first few moments, it can hold their attention and give you enough time to deliver value that can resonate.

Another case where The No-Bull Script can convert higher is

when we are facing industries or job titles in which the stakeholder we want to speak with has either a) very little time, or, b) is in an environment where it's difficult to spend the time we need to make it all the way through the CCF script. The industries, personas, or titles this could apply to include automotive servicing, transportation, doctors, facility managers, operations managers, owner/operators, and others with a workday is mostly spent in an urgent state. This includes individuals we need to speak with who are typically busy doing things that require a percentage of their attention, are not in a seated position and ready to actively listen, or have a short window of time before their next task while we are attempting to have a conversation with them.

Early on at SHP, we called into auto repair shops for one of our clients. We had been using our tried and true CCF, but we were getting hung up on like crazy! We tried to start our nice, conversational approach with them and sure enough, *click!* We would get hung up on right away. We all looked at each other, wondering why this was happening. "How could anyone shut down such a logical script structure!?" We'd ask.

Then, it dawned on us to try a different tack: if we were getting hung up on so soon, then maybe that meant we needed to ever-so-swiftly pack in what we needed upfront to buy ourselves more time.

With that in mind, we said, "Hi, this is Ryan with XYZ Company. Hey, don't hang up!" It was jarring enough that it would actually stop them in their tracks, make them look back and say, "Wait, what is going on here?" and allow us to continue our conversation. We then adopted and evolved this approach of the pattern interrupt into our script structure to deliver as much as possible early in the conversation before following with the NXTS immediately afterward.

The objective of the No-Bull Script is to adapt the conversation strategy to build value quickly and ask for the NXTS early in the conversation. This speaks to meeting the market where they are and adapting your sales process with their buying behaviors. When used in the appropriate scenarios, the No-Bull structure meets prospects where they are, and puts us in their shoes. Understanding our prospect is one of the fundamentals of any marketer or salesperson to begin with, so why shouldn't it apply to script structure?

Dennys Delgado, VP of sales and marketing at SHP, taught me this early in our work together. Dennys has either reconstructed or built the websites for both SHP and Pereus Marketing (Our previous company name!), and has done so with overwhelming impact. The strategy he's implemented to attract people to our website has always been about ensuring the target personas we were looking to connect with would be able to find us and understand what we do based on the words searched or knowledge our prospects had at the time they searched for us. For outbound channels such as cold calling, our strategy is about adapting our message to where our potential customers are mentally, emotionally, and physically. Considering our prospect and the situation they are in allows us as sales developers to adapt and be dynamic to match their needs and provide better understanding and value when moving them from 0 to 1 in the sales development process.

Here is a breakdown of The No-Bull Script Framework. Instead of a QP, Hi, CP, NXTS component format, the components are moved to the following order:

1. QP/CP
2. NXTS/Hi
3. CP 2
4. NXTS 2

1. QUICK PROP & CALLING PROP

In The No-Bull Script, there is a need to hyper focus on the time it takes to move quickly through the value we create here. As we discussed, time and patience can be very short with our target, so we have to dive in quickly to an intro and value that is sharp and crystal clear.

Here is an example No-Bull Script QP/CP for SHP:

QP/CP:

Hi my name is _____ with Superhuman Prospecting. We provide outsourced cold calling and appointment setting for companies like yours and can help you generate between 1 and 100 leads per month to help grow your business.

2. NEXT STEPS & HONE-IN

Since we are assuming this individual is either receiving an overload of calls, is very busy, or is not in a physical location suitable for a full sales conversation, asking for the NXTS as the 2nd step in the conversation can be more impactful in these environments.

The unique part about the No-Bull Script with this component combination is that we have to be ready very quickly for an immediate Hi or *objections and responses* pivot if the prospect rejects the initial request for NXTS. At this point, ask the same question you would in the CCF to get them back into a conversation.

Look back at the Conversion Probability Timeline. While the component order is different, the point is the longer we are on the phone, the better chance we have at converting to the step in the sales process we are looking for. The Hi in this framework brings us back to an adopted CCF script if our first attempt at The No-Bull Script doesn't work.

See the example script language for SHP here:

NXTS/Hi:

I was calling to see if we could schedule a 15 minute call at a later date to see if we can help you grow your business, or at least point you in the right direction. Would you be open to this?

[IF YES]:

[Close]

Great! How is DATE at TIME?

Fantastic. What is your email address and contact info so I can send you an invite and prepare for our consultation?

Great. Look forward to speaking with you then! We'll send you an invite and speak with you on [DATE] at [TIME]!

[IF NO]:

Hi

No problem. Are you using a cold call solution currently to help continue your growth or have you considered it in the past?

3. CALLING PROP 2

If we are this far in The No-Bull Script, the conversation has shifted away from setting up the early NXTS and has moved more towards the CCF. It's also worth noting that if the prospect has answered the Hi, it must be assumed they have given implicit permission to continue the conversation. There is something to be said in these moments about respecting our prospect's time. When we get out what we need to say quickly, even if their response is "no" to our NXTS request, it can still buy you additional precious moments from the other end. The window may be tight, but a slight benefit or feature mentioned could have perked their ear, even if they weren't ready for the highest NXTS on our list.

Moving through the component order as you would in the Hi, the only change might be which key in the VPT you add into the CP. Since you have combined or added some value in the QP/CP in the beginning, you'll want to identify, based upon how the stakeholder responded, whether you should repeat the same value or if you need to move onto something else.

Here is an example of what might be said at SHP:

...so the way it works is we help companies generate leads and appointments for their sales pipeline by making outbound calls and emails to their prospects through campaigns on a month-to-month basis.

- **Differentiating Feature**: We have US-based sales development reps that work for you using the only comprehensive cold call method available from philosophy to frameworks.
- **Tangible Benefit**: We typically generate between 1 to 100 leads per month for our clients depending on the project size and industry
- **Outstanding Accolade**: We have done work for hundreds of SMBs up to companies such as AmerisourceBergen, Moen, Uber, and Amazon

4. NEXT STEPS 2

Finally, once we regroup from the Hi and CP, we ask for the NXTS again. It can sometimes feel like we are pushing the limit, but aiming for two asks is typically the balance between not enough assertion and too much aggression.

NXTS 2:

Now that we've had some time to discuss, would you be open to a phone call at a later date to discuss this further?

The CCF and The No-Bull Script frameworks can seem very similar, but the small nuances can make all the difference. Those first few seconds of a conversation with the stakeholder are crucial, so keeping your ear to the ground to identify how stakeholders or decision makers are reacting early in your sales development calls will help guide you toward one framework or the other.

CHAPTER 24
THE SURVEY SCRIPT

There is a third script framework that emerged from our work at SHP: The Survey Script. In some markets with specific product or service offerings, the CCF and No-Bull Script just don't quite maximize the need at hand. In some situations, The Survey Script framework can help draw interest and qualify better than the other two frameworks.

The Survey Script is a structure designed to create product interest, allure, and exclusivity, with the prospect. This is different than in other frameworks because it is less focused on providing the VPT, and more geared toward provoking thought around the *qualifying questions* being asked of the prospect. In the CCF and No-Bull Script, each possess an aim to identify pain and generate interest throughout the conversation. Their goals also match: sell the NXTS. Additionally, qualifying questions are generally asked after interest is established.

Conversely, the Survey Script's focus is to glean information from the prospect, create a sense of exclusivity in the product (or a perception of gated access), and showcase allure around what the selling company will do with the information.

Products and services that work well with this framework

include some commercial insurance, machinery, new or unique products to market for looking for product feedback or competitive data, commercial real estate investment companies, and others! On the other side of the table, industries receptive to survey script formats are industries such as manufacturing, companies with heavy machinery, e-commerce, architectural or general contracting, commercial property owners, and more. The Survey Script can also be good for calling a current customer base to gather information about their experience or about new products and services on the horizon.

The Survey Script is all about maximizing the conversion of a conversation into next steps that can turn into new business. The H2H cold call component framework for The Survey Script looks like this:

1. QP
2. Hi/NXTS 1
3. QQ (Qualifying Questions)
4. NXTS 2

The NXTS subcomponent of *qualifying questions* is the only piece of the Survey Script puzzle to come out of the primary 4 Core Component alignment. Typically, all four primary components would be the bones; however, in The Survey Script, the objectives are flipped and the conversation prioritizes to a pseudo pre-discovery call with disqualification vibes. Remember, the design is to create allure and exclusivity. By asking questions that could disqualify the prospect, FOMO (Fear of Missing Out) can kick in and give something desired by the prospect.

The first component of The Survey Script Framework is the QP. Generally in The Survey Script, the QP is standard and follows the QP API as aforementioned. The QP is designed to get past the first few seconds and situate the prospect's attention within the right frame. The instruction then is to provide a description of your offering and state a light benefit or feature.

Here's an example from the SHP Survey Script:

1. QP - Quick Prop

Hey [NAME], this is [YOUR NAME] with [YOUR COMPANY NAME]. We provide cold call and appointment setting service to companies such as yours to help generate sales leads so you can grow.

The second component is where our approach differs the most from traditional appointment-setting formats in the CCF and No-Bull Script. In the second component, the Hi and NXTS 1 combine to make a statement with a pause rather than a question. We hold our question for the next component, but replace it with a gap of silence. This implicitly invites a prospect's response without explicitly requesting one.

While we don't cover this psychology much in this book, the general theory is that conversation gaps act as a catalyst for provoking response. By pausing here (which is easier said than done!), we:

- Provide prospects with time to think and digest your prior statement
- Enable prospect engagement
- Withhold a traditional Hone-in question since we will be asking qualifying questions in the following step.

Regardless of whether they engage, attempt to move to the third component to keep the conversation going.

2. Hi/NXTS 1

We've spotted your product/service as a good fit for cold calling and have 5 quick questions to ask to see if you'd qualify for the partnership.

[PAUSE FOR ANY PROSPECT RESPONSE]

Permission granted to continue..

[MOVE TO COMPONENT 3]

No permission to continue..

No problem. Is there a better time to call back to review if you qualify?

[DOCUMENT, SET TIME FOR CALL BACK, END CALL]

Whether implicit or explicit permission is granted after component 2, begin with the first question in the Survey (Qualifying) Questions step. At this juncture, the answers we receive enable similar signs to those when we are in the CCF script. That's because while we have received permission to continue, we haven't necessarily built trust up enough to win a true conversation. As you collect data, thank the prospect and reassure them that the information will help greatly as you transition quickly into the next questions.

The survey should be seamless when done effectively (asking the questions while finishing up any notes from prior answers and documenting current ones as soon as possible). Give prospects an opportunity to express their thoughts, and even offer to "grease the wheels" by suggesting answers that others have given. This can give them a frame of reference while allowing the conversation to seamlessly continue. For instance, question 4 below asks, "How many sales leads or appointments do you need per month?" If the prospect is having trouble answering, you can offer a couple suggestions relevant to them:

"Some of our clients need two appointments per week, or eight per month, while some need more like eight per week, and thirty per month. Are these numbers within range?"

Providing options can jog their thinking, allowing them to

answer quickly and keep the conversation going. As we wind down the questions, we ask for their email address (or confirm the one we already have), since this is vital information for continued follow-up. There is also a higher likelihood they will disclose their info when asked in flow with the others since questions or the topic of conversation. Ensure all answers are written down fully and clarify or confirm as needed. It's always best to maximize the time now rather than attempt to call back later when they may not be available.

3. Survey (QUALIFYING) Questions

1

1) How do you currently work to generate outbound sales leads and appointments for your business?

[WRITE DOWN QUALIFYING QUESTION RESPONSE 1]

2

2) Have you had success with cold calling in the past?

[WRITE DOWN QUALIFYING QUESTION RESPONSE 2]

3

3) How many sales leads and/or appointments do you need per month?

2. [WRITE DOWN QUALIFYING QUESTION RESPONSE 3]

4

1) What markets do you target?

3. [WRITE DOWN QUALIFYING QUESTION RESPONSE 4]

5

2) What is your email address?

4. [WRITE DOWN QUALIFYING QUESTION RESPONSE 5]

The fourth component transitions the conversation from information collection to commitment. At this point, we've asked questions around a topic, which the prospect has answered. The prospect can sometimes infer, based on questions asked, what direction next steps may bring. This can give the prospect a level of confidence and trust in the process. And, as our Conversion Probability Timeline states, the longer we are on a call, the higher chance NXTS are granted. Typically, since one-on-one conversations with decision makers or stakeholders are paramount, asking for an appointment to review answers and fit is optimal. We've found some companies prefer to opt out of an appointment-setting question, while some prefer to require it as a NXTS request at minimum. In other words, an appointment-ask may not be appropriate based on the industry. Simply a quote, review, or recommendation may be sufficient based on sales process, industry standard, or volume.

4. NXTS 2

Thank you! We will take these answers to our team and have some details prepared to see if it's a good fit. When is a good time to review ?

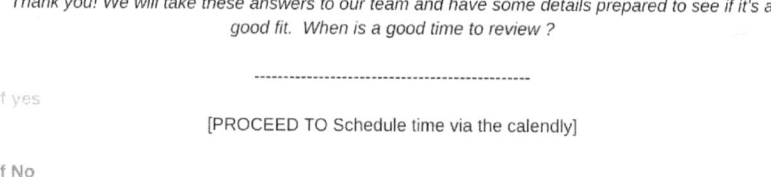

If yes

[PROCEED TO Schedule time via the calendly]

If No

No problem. Can we send you some more info and follow up in the next week or two?

[CONFIRM EMAIL ADDRESS AND SET NURTURE OR WARM and end call]

[WRITE DOWN GENERAL DAY AND TIME AND END CALL]

The Survey Script is the third framework within The H2H Method™ that provides customization to personas and markets either opposed to, stung by, or oversaturated with traditional 0-to-1 appointment-setting cold calls. I wouldn't be surprised if it is not the last format, as new formulations and instances continue to arise as discoveries are made with prospects in the pursuit of perfect conversion rates in our cold calling conversations. By overseeing how your market responds to cold calling, you can test different script formats to optimize. Always be testing!

CHAPTER 25
SCRIPT EXAMPLES BY INDUSTRY

H2H Sales Scripts® and The H2H Method™ for Cold Calling have provided the script frameworks to SHP since its inception. After developing the primary H2H script formats, we've evolved them enough to label, apply, and report back on their successes. Below are four examples from real cold calls made by USA-based cold callers calling from unique industries to different markets. The examples are designed to illuminate the adaptability and impact of the use cases.

In the examples, please note that we measure with metrics used to drive performance and reflect outcomes at SHP. The three primary metrics we track are:

- DM Conversation (Convo) Rate (or, as some call it, DM Connect Rate);
- Appointment Setting Rate, based on the number of conversations we have;
- Appointment Setting Rate on Dials (ASR).

After studying over 300,000 calls in 2020, we found an average DM Convo Rate of 8.32%, an average appointment set on DM Convo Rate of 15.15%, and an average ASR of 1.26%. This study was from data collected and derived from 30 industry origins with multiple industries and personas as targets. Using these numbers as a baseline, you can see how the examples are benchmarked to the averages.

NOTE: Not all scripts in the Script Examples by Industry followed The H2H Method™ exactly. While H2H is the primary driver, some customizations are considered due to SHP client requests.

EXAMPLE 1 - EDUCATION TECHNOLOGY

- **Script Type:** CCF
- **Industry Origin**: Software
- **Industry Target**: Education
- **DM Convo Rate:** 8.93%
- **Appointments Set to DM Convo Rate:** 26.72%
- **ASR**: 2.46%
- **Lead Setting Rate (*appointment, warm, & nurture leads*)**: 4.94%
- **Monthly Campaigns Analyzed**: 7

QP

Hi, this is [YOUR NAME] with [COMPANY NAME]. We build custom outdoor digital escape adventures for schools like yours. Rather than generic icebreakers, tours, or photo scavenger hunts, students just need to download our app and they can play a team-based escape adventure at their location.

Hi

Do you have fun and interactive events that take very little time to plan for your students?

If YES: Great! Glad to hear you see the value in planning events like this for your audience/customers. We are very unique and the only company that can offer these types of events . . . [GO TO CP]

If NO: No problem, and that's exactly why I am reaching out . . . [GO TO CP]

CP

The way it works is we'll build you a custom experience which can be played by hundreds or thousands of players. Teams are outside, running across your location, all competing on one leaderboard for your event.

It's kind of like if Pokemon GO met a team-based escape room. Teams of students will explore campus in a 1-2 hr escape adventure. The storyline is completely customized to campus, highlighting all the things that make it special; it takes less than 30 minutes of administrators' time to set up.

Discovery Questions

1. What activities are you doing currently for orientation?
2. What feedback have you received from orientations in the past?

NXTS

The reason I'm calling is to see if you would be open to a Google Meet call with my CEO to see if this is something that would work for you. Would you be open to this?

How is [WEEKDAY] at [TIME]?

Housekeeping & Qualifying Questions

(HOUSEKEEPING AND QUALIFYING QUESTIONS STEPS REDACTED FROM EXAMPLE)

———

EXAMPLE 2 - IT MSP

- **Script Type:** CCF
- **Industry Origin**: Information Technology
- **Industry Target**: Small to Midsize Businesses (SMB)
- **DM Convo Rate:** 8.55%
- **Appointments Set to DM Convo Rate:** 9.59%
- **ASR:** 0.86%
- **Monthly Campaigns Analyzed:** 21

QP

Hi [DECISION MAKER NAME], this is [YOUR NAME] with [COMPANY NAME]. I'm calling because we understand during this time, you may need to fortify your business' position and growth now more than usual. We're a local provider of managed IT services based right here in [LOCATION], and we're now offering savings of up to 50% on IT services.

Hi

Do you have a local provider of managed services based here in [LOCATION] offering these savings?

If YES: Great! It's good to hear you already see the value in this. This is exactly why I am reaching out. We can often compliment those who have a partner depending . . . [GO TO CP]

If NO: No problem, and that's exactly why I am reaching out . . . [GO TO CP]

CP

. . . So again, we're a local provider of managed services based right here in [LOCATION]. We provide companies with a full-service IT team for less than the cost of a full-time staff IT person.

- **[Differentiating Feature]**: We're local to the [LOCATION] area, so we are immediately accessible for any emergency or critical event.
- **[Tangible Benefit]**: Our pricing is based on the number of users, which can save you up to 50% of what a full-time IT team member would cost.
- **[Outstanding Accolade]**: [GOVT AGENCY #1] is one of our current clients.

Discovery Question

1. How do you manage your IT to remain secure and functional now?

Extended Call Prop [IF NECESSARY/OPTIONAL]

We've also worked with local organizations you might be familiar with such as [BANK #1], [NON-PROFIT #1], [LOCAL BUSINESS #1].

NXTS

The reason I'm calling is to see if you would be open to either a phone call or a face-to-face meeting, at the restaurant of your choice or at your location, with our president, [NAME], to see how we can best work with you, as well as how much you'll save on your IT. Would that work?

Housekeeping & Qualifying Questions

(HOUSEKEEPING AND QUALIFYING QUESTIONS STEPS REDACTED FROM EXAMPLE)

———

EXAMPLE 3 - COMMERCIAL INSURANCE

- **Script Type:** No-Bull Script
- **Industry Origin**: Commercial Insurance
- **Industry Target**: Trucking & Fleet Companies
- **DM Convo Rate:** 15.53%
- **Appointments Set to DM Convo Rate:** 32.34%
- **ASR**: 5.02%

QP/CP

Hi, my name is [YOUR NAME] with [COMPANY NAME]. We know you get a lot of calls, but all we do is insurance for the transportation industry. [SALES REP], our transportation specialist, was looking at your safety report and he has seen something in there and really thinks he can help you reduce your insurance costs.

NXTS/Hi

He wanted me to get a hold of you because he wants to show you what he is seeing. Would you have time this [DAY] at [TIME] to get together with him?

If YES: Great, that time works! We will shoot you an email confirming the date and time. One last thing! In the email, we will also include a list of items we'll need to propose insurance and costs. It's the same stuff that you are used to sending [ITEM 1, ITEM 2, ITEM 3, etc.]. Can you shoot that info back to us prior to the meeting time?

If NO: Oh okay, no problem, have you looked at your truckers' insurance costs recently?

[EMPATHIC RESPONSE, TRANSITION TO CP 2]

CP 2

. . . So we help truckers, and truckers only, reduce their insurance costs the right way through safety. We actually have our own in-house safety program, and we use safety to leverage down your insurance costs.

What's unique about us is we focus on safety as a component of cost reduction, and have helped over 100 companies like yours improve their safety scores and reduce their insurance cost.

Discovery Question

1. Where do you shop for the best rates?

NXTS 2

We may be able to help, but [SALES REP] has your safety report and can show you all the places we shop for best rates and also the safety steps you can take to reduce your costs. Would you be open to speaking with [AE NAME] to see if this is something that would work for you, even if not right now? Would you be open to this?

Housekeeping & Qualifying Questions

(HOUSEKEEPING AND QUALIFYING QUESTIONS STEPS REDACTED FROM EXAMPLE)

———

EXAMPLE 4 - MARKETING TECHNOLOGY

- **Script Type:** The Survey Script
- **Primary Industry Origin**: Software
- **Secondary Industry Origin**: Marketing
- **Primary Industry Target**: Healthcare
- **Secondary Industry Target**: Addiction Treatment Centers (Healthcare)
- **DM Convo Rate:** 5.15%
- **Surveys Set to DM Convo Rate:** 49.5%
- **Surveys Set Rate to Dials**: 2.55%

QP/CP

Hi, this is [YOUR NAME], I'm with [COMPANY NAME]. We're building a database of treatment centers to help them generate more leads. We're doing market research to see how addiction treatment centers choose to do their marketing, and to see if we could help when our platform is ready.

Hi/NXTS 1

Would you be open to answering five questions for a $5 Starbucks gift card to help us learn how we can serve centers like yours better?

If YES: [MOVE TO SURVEY (QUALIFYING) QUESTIONS]

If NO: No problem. Is there a better time to call back to review if you qualify?

[DOCUMENT, SET TIME FOR CALL BACK, END CALL]

Survey (QUALIFYING) Questions

1. What is the primary way you advertise?

[WRITE DOWN QUALIFYING QUESTION RESPONSE 1]

2. What do you typically spend on marketing and advertising?

[WRITE DOWN QUALIFYING QUESTION RESPONSE 2]

3. Where do you have the most success in advertising?

[WRITE DOWN QUALIFYING QUESTION RESPONSE 3]

4. If you are using Google, what keywords do you use for SEO?

[WRITE DOWN QUALIFYING QUESTION RESPONSE 4]

5. Are you interested in joining our database to generate referrals for your facility?

[WRITE DOWN QUALIFYING QUESTION RESPONSE 5]

6. What email address do you want your gift card sent to?

[WRITE DOWN QUALIFYING QUESTION RESPONSE 6]

NXTS 2/Housekeeping

Thank you! We appreciate your feedback, and we'll send you the gift card soon. Would you be open to a call-back once our database is ready to see if it'd be a good fit then?

If YES: Great. We have it noted! And to confirm, your email address is [REPEAT BACK EMAIL ADDRESS]. Thank you. We will call you [SAY TIME PERIOD] to discuss if this is a good fit!

[END CALL]

If NO: No problem. We will send you the gift card shortly and follow up with an email at a later time.

[END CALL]

CHAPTER 26
GATEKEEPERS & OBJECTIONS

At this point in the book, we've covered just about every major part of The H2H Method™ to be dangerous on a cold call! However, there are two missing pieces to the puzzle we wouldn't be able to operate without—Gatekeepers and Objections. While this book highlights the critical steps in the initial conversation between the decision maker or stakeholder and the cold caller, Gatekeepers and Objections can be underrated, highly influential parts to quality cold call conversation success. To keep the focus on the primary stakeholder conversations, I'll only touch on the H2H Gatekeeper and Objections theories in this book with the plan of providing more content in the near future. Regardless, the philosophies and theories can be used in a practical way to further cold call success from these inconspicuous conversation moments.

GATEKEEPER CONVERSATIONS

Gatekeepers, secretaries, assistants, spouses—all those people who appear to hold the keys to decision maker access. We'll use "gatekeepers" as a blanket term for those people who perceivably stand guard to the person you think you want to speak to! Many of these gatekeepers have been and are still looked at as less-than-human peasants that are simply an impediment or wall SDRs have to break through to reach the perceived "decision maker." Furthermore, and more relevant to the twenty-first century, many dialing softwares either have robocalling capabilities or teams of people that make calls on behalf of the SDR. The perception is that gatekeepers are simply an objective and trivial piece to the sales development cold phone call puzzle. The problem is that this creates an overload, friction, and even more resistance to the person on the other end. Over time, the overloading, scamming, and "stonewall" mentality hurts the perception of cold calls from a macro level and crushes potential conversation rates with gatekeepers and decision makers on a call-to-call level.

I get it. Gatekeepers are a tough part of the cold caller role. I'm sure many would take a scrappy decision maker over a nice gatekeeper any day of the week. Gatekeepers can be daunting, so I understand why so many callers want to avoid, break down, or push them over, but this is not the highest converting approach, let alone the human-to-human way! We can't hold these approaches if we want to build trust and convert at the highest level. And as our strategy lays out, potential customers aren't just the stakeholders and decision makers, they are also the gatekeepers! Robo-dialers and teams of dialers meant to get the decision maker on the phone before passing the line to the SDR can have serious consequences from expensive data to reach these ever-crucial decision makers and stakeholders. Moreover, the most common misconception in understanding gatekeepers is these very people can many times be stakeholders or decision makers, themselves!

If the goal is to maintain and push the envelope in highest performance while never losing trust with potential customers, then we have to assume every gatekeeper is a prospect that might find value in what we offer. There is an H2H strategy that achieves our goal within gatekeeper conversations. Before sharing, I have to reiterate our change of mindset! By remembering gatekeepers are humans as well, they are in many ways the key to more decision maker conversations; treating every gatekeeper with respect, even if the call can feel tense, is a fundamental truth that must be accepted before moving forward. If you can't accept this, you'll still get through gatekeepers. You'll still have "wins," you'll simply lose the possibility of highest conversion in the long term.

Ultimately, it's up to you. You certainly don't have to choose this route. There are others out there that prove success. Many sales people have made their money pushing. The difference is The H2H Method™ for Cold Calling provides values and structure to optimize conversion regardless of what is faced in cold calling conversations. I understand gatekeeper conversations can be difficult; I've faced many. One of the primary responsibilities for most gatekeepers when they were hired is *literally* to fend off pesky salespeople. Yes, you are their prey and that's why many conversations can start off so abrasive. They are trying to distill down the purpose of your call so they know whether it's "safe" to patch in the decision maker. You realize why many try to skip this conversation now, right? You are in an instant hole, and it's not even your fault. Because of your position, you have to be extra nimble with techniques, reactions, and responses to gatekeepers, because in a moment's notice they can deny requests, and you're left with a dial tone.

So while there are many techniques and ideas for getting to your decision maker (both H2H and NOT), we have observed these techniques can be boiled down to two primary tactics trained to optimize gatekeeper conversations to maximize connections with decision makers or stakeholders. Choosing which one depends on your industry, target market, offering, and even to the individual gatekeeper personality with whom you are speaking. We have identified these two primary methods called the *pass through* and *engage*.

Pass Through

The *pass through* is designed for those conversations encountering the following situations:

- When you know with 90% certainty or more the correct name of the decision maker or stakeholder you are looking for
- For those industries that are saturated from cold phone calls
- For those industries that have been instructed by the decision makers or stakeholders to not accept solicitation calls
- For those gatekeeper personalities that are difficult to engage in conversation

Here is what a *pass through* gatekeeper conversation might look like:

---PASS THROUGH--

SDR: Hello, is _[DM FIRST NAME]_ available?

GK: And what is your name?

SDR: [SAY YOUR FIRST NAME ONLY]

GK: And who are you with?

SDR: [SAY SIMPLIFIED VERSION OF COMPANY NAME ONLY IF APPLICABLE (ie. for Superhuman Prospecting, say "Superhuman")]

GK: Okay, and what is the call regarding?

SDR: [STATE GENERAL INDUSTRY AREA ONLY (ie. for Superhuman Prospecting, say "Sales", or, "Marketing")]

GK:
1) Okay, let me pass you through...

In observing the script, you'll see that by answering in as few words as possible, you exude confidence and purpose. We don't have to share our life story or ask about theirs this early in the conversation. By abbreviating our language here, we are focusing on efficiency. When first speaking with a gatekeeper, we can eliminate waste in our conversation by minimizing words that build no value or don't help us get to the decision maker faster. Since we don't know how much influence this gatekeeper has, starting off with minimal language gives us time to read and understand what type of gatekeeper this person may be! For instance, is the person simply a switchboard operator? Are they a secretary for multiple decision makers within an organization? What about a personal assistant? A spouse of the decision maker? A stakeholder? We really don't know. So being efficient *early* in the gatekeeper conversation will usually place us in a position for the best decisions to be made as we find out more information throughout the call.

You see, the strategy isn't to lie, strong arm, or trick the gatekeeper into passing us on to someone we want to speak with. First, this would not check-out with our H2H selling values. Second, if we don't reach the person we'd like to speak with in this call, the call back might be even tougher because their senses will be alerted to your nonsense. And third and most importantly, *the person we are calling very well might be the stakeholder or decision maker we want to speak with!*

Imagine that. We unknowingly have the right person on the phone who could quite possibly be the next big investment and partnership in your product, but because we said "Please pass me to [NAME] because we have an appointment scheduled right now" when there was no appointment, we have decimated trust and are left on the doorstep packing to our next call.

Engage

The *engage* method is virtually the opposite of *pass through*, as it focuses on utilizing the opportunity to treat the gatekeeper as a stakeholder, selling them first on the value, with the end goal of them passing you on or taking a meeting themselves as a viable stakeholder in the decision. In addition, we often might not know who the true decision maker is, or at least, if the gatekeeper is actually a stakeholder that has significant influence on a purchasing decision.

Here is an example of the *engage* method in practice in a possible script for SHP:

---ENGAGE--

SDR: Hello, is _[DM FIRST NAME]_ available?

GK: And what is the call regarding?

SDR: Absolutely. I am wondering if you can help me. I am with Superhuman Prospecting and we have a US-based team that provides cold calls to help generate sales leads and appointments for your business so it can grow. Are you the right person to speak with?

GK:
1) Actually, I handle this side of the business, so yes...

[GO TO DM SCRIPT]

2) Hmm, no, that would be [SAYS DM NAME]

SDR: No problem. Could I speak with [DM NAME]?

GK: Yes, please hold...

[GK PASSES YOU TO DM - GO TO DM SCRIPT]

The first reason to *engage* the gatekeeper is that we are committing to spending more time with them. Remember if the *pass through* is meant to be efficient, *engaging* the gatekeeper is first designed to spend more time with them to discover who the right person might be. Secondly, this practice enables the gatekeeper to be treated as a stakeholder or decision maker. By phrasing our *engage* calling proposition with features and benefits, we can gauge their interest or stake by how they respond. As seen in the example script, based on how the gatekeeper (GK) responds, the SDR will either continue to speak with the gatekeeper as a stakeholder, or, the SDR will confirm the name of the person they should be speaking with and continue down that path.

The gatekeeper conversation is probably the most dreaded conversation in sales prospecting, but it can also be one of the most important, as it can be influential in the number of decision maker/stakeholder conversations you have. The more decision maker/stakeholder conversations you have, the better chance you have of setting true appointments and generating more opportunity. Unlike so many of your colleagues in the twenty-first century, *do not* underestimate the importance of the gatekeeper! They might be holding the key to a trusted relationship with that business right in front of your face! Don't overlook what could be underneath your nose—you may never get that chance again! Respect the position of the gatekeeper and watch conversations and trust rise.

OBJECTIONS AND RESPONSES

We call it "objections and responses" rather than "objections and rebuttals" because the issues prospects bring up about moving to the next step aren't always objections to be rebutted, pushed over, combatted, or gotten through. We define an objection as any level of *"no,"* resistance, or slowing of the sales process toward selling *next steps.* Typically, we have established these in moving the decision maker further towards a sale. In addition, we sometimes have to consider their disapproval more like FAQs rather than objections. It helps us to actively listen and answer objections to moving to *next steps* while building trust.

In twenty-first-century human-to-human selling scenarios, we recommend two strategies underlying any response that enables trust and helps work back towards *next steps*:

1. Empathize

Help prospects understand that you heard them. You don't necessarily have to use boilerplate rebuttals such as "I understand," or "I can see where you are coming from,." as much as you should try to communicate that you hear them in some way—whether it's restating what they said, clarifying the value of the next step, and/or mirroring their emotion through tone and pace of voice, empathizing is more than lip service. It's more about diffusing, listening, and responding with value. It also helps with using those few seconds to collect your thoughts for a precise response. Jeb Blount writes about this in his book, *Objections*. He calls them *ledges*. He says:

In fast-moving situations, to effectively deal with disruptive emotions, you need only a millisecond for your logical brain to wake up and tell the emotional brain to stand down. This allows you to regain your poise and control of the conversation…a ledge can be a statement, acknowledgement, agreement, or question. [1]

You've heard this before. "I completely understand," or "a lot of others I've spoken to have said something similar." The ledge allows you those few microseconds to collect yourself and respond appropriately based upon what they said. Empathy can be displayed in a number of ways, so it can take reading the prospect, the situation, and their emotions to determine the best way to respond.

2. Slow down *their* buying process perception

When making intentional moves to slow down the buying process in the mind of the prospect, we can help the decision maker realize the cold call is less about a "sale" for us to take from them and more about educating, providing value, or helping. This is pivotal in helping move an individual from that 0-to-1 business relationship mind space, let alone a sales pipeline phase. Repeat that out loud! It is so important to build trust, especially in objections, with the purpose to "slow down the buying process in the mind of the prospect." So many objections are reinforced in the prospect feeling they're dealing with a sales call and not actually talking about their use case of your product or service. The remedy is communicating as quickly and swiftly as possible when the pressure is off the sale. When they are confident we are not going to take their money right now, or they sense we aren't looking for them to sign on the dotted line by the end of the call, we can start to win back trust. Finding these things help identify common ground with the prospect. These are the types of reactions that really help slow the buying process in their mind, which allows us to speed up trust with them so we can continue the next steps. Here is an example:

Decision Maker (DM): "We can't take on anything new right now."

Immaculate Cold Caller: "[DM NAME] no problem, really. I understand. While we'd love your partnership sometime down the line, and we're not looking to have you sign anything right now. If we're able to set up some time in the next couple of days or weeks, at least we would have an opportunity to share with you how we think this could help you. It would also give you some time to think about this to make the best decision for your business."

Slowing down the perception of the sales cycle in their mind eases their instincts. They sense we as sales people are not trying to do the deal at this moment. This helps the prospect realize they make the decision when you're ready, but the next step can really help provide you with the best information.

These objection strategies, just like in our Trust Umbrella, give us context in how to use our tactical responses when facing objections. But what type of objections are there? When analyzing these at face value, we find three types:

- Real Objections
- Concerns
- Disguised Interest

Real Objections are those conversation scenarios where the

prospect blocks your sales process for legitimate "no" reasons. These will reveal prospects' perceived non-interest or non-willingness to move forward with any type of next step. This can come in the form of, "We're too busy for something like this right now," "I don't have time for this," "I'm not interested," etc. These can generally feel the worst when you hear them, because you can feel you are now entering a deeper hole to dig out of. Whether this is true or not is yet to be seen, because some Real Objections are simply an emotional response that needs to be diffused rather than a genuine and well-thought-out rejection of your offering. Either way, building muscle memory in the response through practice and repetition positions yourself for a win when facing Real Objections.

Concerns then, are when the prospect has familiarity with your offering, product, or service, but has come to a roadblock before a decision. They have either heard about your service, investigated a product like yours before, or used it and had a less-than-optimal experience. So if they say something like, "I tried something similar, but it didn't work the way I was hoping," then there is a difference between this and a Real Objection. The reason is because they aren't necessarily opposed to your specific sales conversation and offer yet. There is potential energy there in the frustration. They may feel a certain way about your product or service, but it can be wrapped up in a desire for it to work. This can often present really awesome opportunities for you to respond appropriately and encourage them to that next step.

Disguised Interest objections are those any salesperson should want to hear! Disguised Interest objections are typically questions or statements that reflect more information or discussion desired by the prospect. These are not always obvious because they can be masked as objections or concerns, but really, they just want to know more. So if they ask, "How much does this cost," then this could be a sign they have considered this, have thought about it, are curious, and/or are interested! Seems like an easy one to deal with, right? No! Not all the time. In fact, the impact can be such that we as salespeople can feel overly excited and begin pitch-punching these prospects! The key is in restraining ourselves, remembering our primary cold call strategies, and responding in a way that helps them see that an appointment to discuss this type of question is best!

There are different ways to categorize and label objections, as many sales improvement greats have already done. But why we identify them as such here is because they can offer hints as to what lies behind the "no," giving us confidence and direction with what to say next to optimize conversion while building trust with our potential customer. Below are some templated examples of all three objection types and possible responses to help move you to the NXTS! (Use these and customize based on your value prop and offering as needed.)

Real Objections

Objection 1: *We are happy with our current process.*
Response 1: *That is great to hear! And as I mentioned, we can most likely compliment what you are currently doing and we are different from most companies. We are the only company who [list Differentiating Feature]. Not many others are doing this for companies like yours right now.*

Objection 2: *We don't want to bring on anything new right now.*
Response 2: *Absolutely! And while we'd appreciate your business at some point, right now we just want to help you learn about the topic to see if this could work for you.*

Objection 3: *We don't have the money right now.*
Response 3: *We understand and fortunately our objective isn't to have anyone sign any contracts today. The appointment I talk about is just to help you learn. This way, you would at least know how much it would cost for when the finances make more sense.*

Concerns

Concern 1: *We had a bad experience with a similar company.*
Response 1: *I'm sorry to hear that and that probably doesn't help our case, does it? I completely understand your pain, and we have designed our company to help eliminate those experiences that many have had in our industry.*

Concern 2: *This is probably expensive.*
Response 2: *Well, I am happy to share our price on a demo if that makes sense. The goal of my call is to help you see if we can help first, and then talk about price. If not, we may be able to point you in the right direction.*

Disguised Interest

Interest 1: *We don't know how this works.*
Response 1: *I completely understand and that is one of the reasons why we're calling. If we can schedule some time, we can share how it works and identify how this may help you, whether or not you actually choose us.*

Interest 2: *I would use your product/service, but I don't make the final decision.*
Response 2: *That's okay. This is the first time we are speaking. The goal would be to set up some time to help you learn a little bit more so you can see if it would even make sense to share with that person.*

While these aren't all the full list of Real Objections, Concerns, and Disguised Interest objection examples, they reflect common and initial intent from prospects. They also provide "H2H approved" responses to get the conversation back on track towards the top NXTS.

Notice on each of these objection examples, empathizing is just one part of the overall picture. "That's great to hear," or "absolutely," are ways to help the individual you're speaking with under-stand that you heard them and know what issue they're dealing with. This is how one's personality might most naturally express their agreement with the other, but using your own words here enables authenticity. These ledge statements also give us time to breathe and collect thoughts before responding. Like we've stated as well, cold call empathy is simply slowing down the process in the mind of the prospect. By slowing down the buying process in their mind, we're able to build trust in our process again. Trust is so crucial in these moments because the conversation can go south if we aren't able to respond acutely and accurately. Again, if an objection is defined as any resistance to move toward next steps we have established in moving the decision maker further towards a sale, then we have to understand why that is and help reiterate value by empathizing and slowing down the buying process in their mind.

———

Now that we've covered objections, let's clarify the difference between an objection vs product knowledge. We are assuming questions from prospects about the product or service itself will require technical product or service knowledge responses. These are separate from objection responses for the conversation here. All objections in this dialogue are those appropriate for the cold call appointment-setting phase. While not ironclad, the Objections and Responses as classified here are related to the general product features, benefits, accolades, and separate sales process. Many times, these product question scenarios are actually a form of interest rather than disinterest, so it's essential we either be prepared with an answer that provides value, or at a minimum, know how to respond quickly to set up next steps. For example, if a decision maker or stakeholder has a question about pricing such as "How much does it cost?" with SHP, we might focus on a ques-tion response that sounds something like this:

"That's a great question. The way it works is we price by the activity,

and there are bolt-on options, such as inside sales support and prospecting data research. It would take a few more minutes to explain in detail. Would you be open to a call with our AE, [NAME], to go over this with you?"

Notice we didn't explain pricing in depth here. Even if we knew, and we were the AE, let's not forget the primary strategies of a cold phone call! Our objectives are to spark interest, diffuse the *salesperson stigma*, and sell the *next steps*, not the product or service itself—not yet. Remembering this will enable the decision maker and would-be new prospect to develop a curiosity and opportunity for the AE (whether that is you or someone else) to present value when the prospect has most of their *salesperson stigma* diffused on another call. So much of the cold phone call can be emotionally charged (both positively and negatively), so letting the heat simmer for the appropriate next step will enable both parties to be ready.

On the other hand, if the SDR does not know or is protected from certain information about a product or service, it's best to have a catch-all statement that helps the decision maker understand the answer will be provided in the next conversation or next step. Many SDRs and sales leaders fear a scenario where the SDR does not have the knowledge for the answer; however, many decision makers understand that not every rep calling is going to know everything. While a base level of knowledge is absolutely critical, it is almost never required or necessary for an SDR to have all the answers as an AE would. And as we covered, sparking the interest is the goal. Here is how an answer to the same pricing question ("How much does it cost?) might go at SHP:

"Well, that is a great question and very common. That's exactly why I am calling. We wanted to call and see if you'd be open to speaking with our AE, [NAME], to explain this a bit more when we both have more time. We dig into what your needs are and how the pricing can fit your budget and goals."

Even if the decision maker requests this from the SDR, there are several ways to overcome this question. It is never bad to be transparent about your position with the company. You can say something like "that is above my pay grade," or, "I actually don't know the pricing." There is no shame in the position of an SDR. I say it all the time on my client's' campaigns when I prospect for them. Understanding the objectives on a cold phone call to know how to set up the best next steps as it relates to your company's pipeline strategy is the intent. I only ask whether you are an AE or SDR cold phone calling, ensure you are following the pipeline strategy that best sets up the next part of the process.

Objections & Responses can go so much deeper, but for the sake of your attention, the focus of this book, and more content coming, this summary should give you enough insight into the way The H2H Method™ approaches Objections and Responses to them. Responding to objections is a trained skill, but if the foundational theories aren't built in first, they can turn into bad habits. Bad habits can morph into aggression, passiveness, missed opportunities, and a lack of trust felt from prospects. Reflecting on, thinking about, and beginning to use the philosophies here will build a foundation for learning how to spark enough interest in what you do to bring them to next steps without losing trust.

VOICEMAILS

I've wrestled with the idea of adding a voicemail section to this book. Like the topics of Gatekeepers and Objections, I wasn't going to add a significant amount of content, but at a minimum provide some strategy and tactics. After reviewing our data and results, the confidence in a method that works is purely anecdotal. No significant empirical evidence has been collected. That is primarily due to a process function at SHP limiting the collection and conversion data to prove the method's voicemail efficacy. That said, I'm confident voicemail return dials simply happen with positive outcomes. If you don't leave a message, call-back conversations are not only fewer, but less quality when they do occur. If you are clear with who you are and how you can help, it is not only more beneficial to the prospect, but to you as the salesperson. In addition, elements of building trust without deception is evident in any voicemail prescribed by H2H. Any mystery, illusion, or bait and switch is off the table. Sales transparency and clear communication is evident. Diffusing the *salesperson stigma* and building trust remain.

Insights on voicemails may be available at another time in a future publication, so be on the lookout for how to leave compliant, relevant, and impactful voicemails with an ROI.

SECTION FIVE
EVOLVING FUTURES
WITH H2H

CHAPTER 27
H2H TRUST IS CONSTANT, BUT MARKETS ARE NOT

Congrats for making it through the most systematic and comprehensive cold call methodology book on the shelves! It shows your commitment to the craft, and you have the mindset required for modern sales conversations. Something unique about this script methodology is it *commits* to a structural design. The design is shaped by belief, philosophy, strategy, and efficacy. As we drill deeper, things can easily become more nuanced and customized for ranging personality types; however, the more data we review, the more we can define a science with the art. The design of The H2H Method™ isn't invincible, as the bones of the conversation structures are simply a reflection of how potential human buyers interact most positively towards sales development conversation pipeline movement from 0 to 1 in the BRT. As we've touched on, the sales process is symbiotic with the buying process. The salesperson sets the goals, and the buyer follows at the pace where trust and value are met. When considering cold phone conversations in the twenty-first century, the same rule applies. As the profession of sales evolves, sales processes may change slightly; however, the buyer is ultimately dictating the tone, pace, and relationship until the sales goal is met. While market change will always impact the sales process, the rate at which cold phone conversation structures change will be slower than other channels where technology is involved. For instance, cold phone call structures made 15 years ago are similar to those made and those that are successful today. With the exception of some changes in data, openers, additions to sales person vocabulary, mirroring, entrainment, and emotional intelligence, structure and delivery are at a similar pace and length relative to the market then as they are now.

On the other hand, the cold email strategy and process have evolved significantly in the last 15 years compared to its cold phone call counterpart. When email prospecting first emerged, opens and replies could be won with 500- to 1000-word cold whitepaper email deliveries with little relevance or personalization. Fast forward to 2023, and the collective recommended amount of words in a single cold email is under 150 words and optimally, 75 or fewer. In addition, relevance and personalization requirements for success are at an all-time high. Without knowing challenges or issues of the prospective title or company, or the history and personal things about the prospect, cold email prospecting can be daunting with opens and replies met with silence or unsubscribes.

These lessons around adapting human conversation and digital communication circle a similar yet larger concept studied for ages —continuous improvement. While market awareness sparks adaptation, so does the focus on constant process and outcome optimization. One of my favorite parts of selling is the impossible ideal to achieve 100% conversion on all metrics. The objective creates unlimited questions that provide grounds for infinite growth. Regarding the topic of cold calling, the following macro questions could be asked:

- How do I find perfect data that reaches stakeholders or decision makers every time?
- How does one reach 100% of stakeholders/decision makers from our calling efforts?
- How do you convert 100% of the decision maker connections or conversations you have into desired next steps?

The questions then get deeper and deeper. As results are collected, the steps cycle and cycle and cycle. The Deming Institute identifies the continuous improvement cycle as the Deming Wheel, or the Deming Cycle, an integrated learning-improvement model.[1]

1. **Plan**—This step is identifying a goal or purpose, formulating a theory, defining success metrics and putting a plan into action
2. **Do**—Components of a plan are implemented
3. **Study**—Outcomes from implementation are monitored
4. **Act**—Integrates learning by the process which can be used to adjust Plan

Rinse and repeat! Applying continuous improvement at set intervals provides real data to compare with projected/expected data. The answers are in the gaps. The H2H Method™ utilizes continuous improvement to achieve greater success by executing call plans, reviewing results, notes, recordings, and dialogue with callers. Reflection turns to filling a new need based on areas of improvement. A new plan is created and calls begin again. Each time, the relevance of the product is more refined, the target market is more clear, the messaging resonates better, and the SDR is more attuned to high-performance conversations.

While human-to-human conversation may change slower than digital communication, a continuous improvement mindset has no bounds. Macro changes in the market minimally impact the opportunity for macro improvements to our day-to-day, week-to-week, month-to-month, or quarter-to-quarter cold call performance. It's one of the most beautiful aspects of the art and science of the cold call. As we've seen, conversions are generally small in cold calling (i.e., 8.32% DM Convo Rate and 1.26% ASR) when using raw phone number data, separate from pre-called data or people called previously to identify only those who pick up the phone. Some would interpret these numbers as irrelevant and not worth the investment to market in the channel. I see these numbers as a blue ocean of discovery, even when using raw data. At the time of this writing, some of the best SHP callers are holding a 10% DM Convo Rate, 20% ASR on Convos, and over a 2% ASR on Dials across a diverse set of industry campaigns. But they didn't start there. Daily, weekly, monthly, they are reviewing their work; making adjustments based on their improvement needs, and then executing, and repeating the process. The incremental improvements look like leaps over the long term. This process is continuous improvement at work, and the byproduct is the H2H Evolution. We evolve and become better with the process. With better processes, there is more opportunity for growth and improvement in our outcomes. Trust is the foundation to building relationships, and continuous improvement is the foundation to highest performance. The two are different, but not mutually exclusive. The two ideals work together to create value for our prospects more powerfully than if the two were working separately.

CONCLUSION

If you are practicing professional selling in the modern era, you are contributing to the advancement of the sales profession at some level. It doesn't matter if you are a sales development representative, account executive, sales manager, director, sales engineer, VP, or entrepreneur just getting started. I hope others, you, and I can advance the sales profession together by inspiring future sales people to find not only efficacy, but more importantly pride, confidence, and purpose in the craft. Anyone on this journey in the modern era is contributing to a massive momentum shift in the sales vocation. Sales professionals are unraveling outdated unethical techniques, listening to the buyer, and are influencing them in a way that is helpful, rather than regretful, for prospects and customers alike.

After years of experimentation, analysis, and refinement, our confidence turns to the data-driven outcomes as our primary "proof-in-the-pudding" source for efficacy in this methodology. Not only will it be refined as we test new techniques, strategies, and philosophies, it will also be changing due to shifts in the market. H2H was developed from the bad taste in prospects' mouths from salespeople of a past era. So as we listen to the market, the script needs to adapt to them to serve them better. By putting in the effort through blood, sweat, and tears to maintain a keen awareness of prospect wants, needs, and behaviors, salespeople are closer to the heartbeat of real-time buyer behavior.

Finally, The H2H Method™ continues beyond this book. As I write this, I can foresee the need for a methodology update, a skills and application series to optimize conversions, and new applications to The H2H Method™ in a wide range of arenas where people, organizations, and results meet. In the 21st century, where unethical sales practices creep, digitalization anchors, AI & Chat GPT usage multiplies, and general machine-to-human interaction proliferates, the need to not just rekindle, but advance human-to-human connection is desperately needed to keep relationships and trust at the base of a new era in marketing and sales. If you can hold onto a glimmer of this truth, then I will see you on the journey we are all on to impact the market with trust through human-to-human interaction.

ACKNOWLEDGMENTS

Who do I thank for a technical book on cold calling? Or, maybe the question is, who would want to be thanked? Cold calling, in fact, can be a thankless task. But without it, businesses would not be built, served, or better off.

I'm grateful for the opportunity to be a cold calling journeyman, but it wouldn't be without those backing me to give me the confidence to pursue such a daunting and gritty career, manifesto, and book.

Ben and Karah Davies, thank you for seeing the good in this cause from the early days. Thank you for being friends, sages, supporters, and clients.

Dennys Delgado, thank you for sticking with the crazy idea of offering cold calling as a business model. You saw it from day one and are owed credit for believing in it through the massive wins and equally as enormous challenges. I'm starting to think this level of character building we've experienced couldn't have been found in most other businesses.

SHP Team, this book would not be possible without your belief in the mission to reinvent the cold caller in modern sales development. Your commitment, consistency, and positivity is unmatched. We are improving so rapidly together that every new day I see us as the next best version of ourselves. The effort and results you place your blood, sweat, and tears into have provided clients new business opportunities, you and your families' consistent work, and the ingredients needed to write this book.

Steve and Julie Pereus, thank you for supporting my quests, as deranged, honorable, or futile as they may seem. I seem to be willing to do things with more risk because I know with 100% confidence I have a crash pad in both of you to bring me back, even if on life support.

Rex Biberston I'm calling it now. We will one day work together on something when the time is right. The future business venture is waiting for us out there somewhere! As a past competitor in the outsourced sales space, I've respected, learned from, and appreciated your smooth, seamless, methodical approach that always just seems to make sense. Thank you for all the conversations the last few years. I leave our calls pondering for days.

NOTES

FRONT MATTER

1. Schoonmaker, Thelma, ed. 2013. The Wolf of Wall Street. Directed by Martin Scorsese.

1. THE PROBLEM

1. Collins, Jim, and Morten T Hansen. 2011. Great by Choice: Uncertainty, Chaos, and Luck?: Why Some Thrive Despite Them All. New York, NY: Harper Audio. P. 77.
2. "Use Pattern Interrupts to Increase Sales." n.d. www.customgrowth.sandler.com. Accessed June 20, 2023. https://www.customgrowth.sandler.com/blog/2019/08/pattern-interrupts-increase-sales.

2. WHAT IS THE H2H METHOD™ FOR COLD CALLING?

1. "Definition of Philosophy." In Merriam-Webster Dictionary, June 21, 2023. https://www.merriam-webster.com/dictionary/philosophy.
2. "Philosophy Definition - Google Search," n.d. https://www.google.com/search?q=philosophy+definition.
3. "Strategy Definition - Google Search," n.d. https://www.google.com/search?q=strategy+definition.
4. "Tactic Definition - Google Search," n.d. https://www.google.com/search?q=tactic+definition.
5. "Technique Definition - Google Search," n.d. https://www.google.com/search?q=technique+definition
6. "Method Definition - Google Search," n.d. https://www.google.com/search?q=method+definition.

5. WHAT CLASSIC "POOR SALES ETHICS" LOOKS LIKE

1. AZFamily.com. "Phoenix police bust telemarketing ring that scammed seniors out of $40 million." October 2, 2019.

13. THE BUSINESS RELATIONSHIP TIMELINE (BRT)

1. "Merriam-Webster Dictionary." 2020. Merriam-Webster.com. 2020.https://www.merriam-webster.com/dictionary/cold%20call.

16. A STRATEGY SESSION

1. Jackson, Eric. "Sun Tzu's 31 Best Pieces Of Leadership Advice." Forbes, May 23, 2014. https://www.forbes.com/sites/ericjackson/2014/05/23/sun-tzus-33-best-pieces-of-leadership-advice/?sh=216a25f45e5e.

18. HUMAN 2 HUMAN SALES VALUES

1. Jeb Blount. 2017. Sales EQ : How Ultra-High Performers Leverage Sales-Specific Emotional Intelligence to Close the Complex Deal. Hoboken, New Jersey: John Wiley & Sons, Inc., p. 33.
2. Goleman, Daniel. *Emotional Intelligence: Why It Can Matter More Than IQ.* Random House Publishing Group, 2005. p. 117.

20. H2H SELLING CHARACTERISTICS

1. "British Library." n.d. Www.bl.uk. https://www.bl.uk/people/albert-mehrabian#:~:text=Drawing%20on%20the%20combined%20findings.
2. Goleman, Daniel. Emotional Intelligence: Why It Can Matter More Than IQ. Random House Publishing Group, 2005. p. 97.

22. CONSULTATIVE CONVERSATION FRAMEWORK (CCF)

1. Cialdini, Robert B. (1984) 2016. Influence: The Psychology of Persuasion. Blackstone Audio, Incorporated. P. 23, 29.
2. Cuban, Mark. 2011. How to Win at the Sport of Business : If I Can Do It, You Can Do It. New York, NY: Diversion Books, A Division Of Diversion Publishing Corp. p. 67.

26. GATEKEEPERS & OBJECTIONS

1. Jeb Blount. 2018. Objections!: The Ultimate Guide to Mastering the Art and Science of Getting Past No. Hoboken, New Jersey: Wiley. P. 76.

27. H2H TRUST IS CONSTANT, BUT MARKETS ARE NOT

1. Deming Institute. 2021. "PDSA Cycle." Https://Deming.org/. 2021.https://deming.org/explore/pdsa/.

www.ingramcontent.com/pod-product-compliance
Lightning Source LLC
Chambersburg PA
CBHW060828220526
45466CB00003B/1022